Comprehension  **4 Teachers' Handbook**

Contents

MALVERN PRIMARY SCHOOL

Part one

Part two

PART ONE

Introduction

To develop as effective readers, pupils should be taught to:
- read accurately, fluently and with understanding;
- understand and respond to the texts they read;
- read, analyse, and evaluate a wide range of texts, including literature from the English literary heritage and from other cultures and traditions.
(Revised National Curriculum for English in England and Wales, General requirements for English, 1995)

Learning to read accurately and with discrimination becomes increasingly important as pupils move through their education ... [Pupils] should be helped to develop their own tastes in imaginative literature and non-fiction and at the same time to gain confidence in writing and speaking about them ... The importance of meaning should be stressed at all stages ...
(Scottish 5-14 English Language Curriculum, June 1991)

Pupils should develop the ability to read, understand and engage with various types of text for enjoyment and learning.
(Revised Northern Ireland Curriculum, 1996)

Key Comprehension comprises five Pupils' Books and five accompanying Teachers' Handbooks, aimed at Key Stage 1/Primary 2-3, Lower Key Stage 2/Primary 4-5, Upper Key Stage 2/Primary 6, and more able pupils in Year 6/Primary 7. The series helps to prepare pupils for the Reading Comprehension components of the national Standard Assessment Tasks/National Tests (Scotland). The series may also be used to prepare pupils for the comprehension components of 11+ entry tests in English to grammar schools and independent schools.

The Key Comprehension Starter Book is aimed at pupils in Years 1 and 2/Primary 2-3 and is targeted at National Curriculum Levels 2-3, Scottish 5-14 Curriculum Level A and Northern Ireland Curriculum Levels 1-2.

Book 1 prepares pupils in Year 2 for Reading Comprehension Tests at Key Stage 1/pupils in Primary 3 for the National Tests for infants. It is targeted at National Curriculum Levels 2-4, Scottish 5-14 Curriculum Level A and Northern Ireland Curriculum Levels 1-3.

Book 2 is aimed at pupils in Years 3 and 4/Primary 4-5 and is targeted at National Curriculum Levels 3-5, Scottish 5-14 Curriculum Levels B-C and Northern Ireland Curriculum Levels 2-4.

Book 3 prepares pupils in Years 5 and 6 for the Reading Comprehension Tests at Key Stage 2/pupils in Primary 6-7 for the National Tests for juniors. It is targeted at National Curriculum Levels 3-6, Scottish 5-14 Curriculum Levels C-D, and Northern Ireland Curriculum Levels 3-5.

Book 4 comprises more demanding reading comprehension material for more able pupils in Year 6/Primary 7. It is targeted at those pupils likely to reach the highest levels in the Reading Comprehension Tests at Key Stage 2 or the National Tests for juniors in Scotland.

Structure and components

Key Comprehension Book 4 contains twenty-three self-contained Units of work. Each Unit consists of a passage of text followed by a series of questions which test the children's understanding of the text.

The texts are taken from a wide range of sources, and are lively and stimulating. Care has been taken to reflect the pupils' own experience and to engage their interest. In accordance with Curriculum guidelines, the genres represented include modern and well-established children's fiction, poetry, drama, autobiography, information texts, and transactional material.

The questions are designed to encourage close and accurate reading of the texts and to foster an understanding of implicit as well as explicit meaning. The activities gradually become more demanding as the book progresses. The pupils' ability to skim and to scan, to order and to summarise, to pinpoint and to synthesise information is thus developed throughout the book.

For each Unit, the Teachers' Handbook provides the answers to the questions, a breakdown of the comprehension skills tested in the activity, a suggested mark scheme and a range of ideas for extension work. These extension activities are often open-ended and offer a range of written assignments in a variety of genres, comprehension questions of greater complexity, and related language work.

The Teachers' Handbook also contains a commentary on the range of reading strategies that are needed to develop comprehension skills, National Curricula correlation information, pupil and class record sheets and a Bibliography containing details of the sources of texts for further reading.

How to use Key Comprehension

Units are arranged in order of gradually increasing difficulty and, generally speaking, are intended to be tackled in the order arranged. However, each Unit is self-contained to allow flexibility so teachers may choose to take some Units out of order if a particular topic, genre or question form is relevant to current class work.

Book 4 meets the needs of high-achieving pupils who are expected to gain a high level in English for their age. Texts and questions are linguistically and conceptually challenging. Pupils will probably prefer to tackle the Units with the minimum of teacher intervention, but it is often helpful if the teacher talks through the activity first and explains exactly what it is that they are being asked to do.

Although a prolonged discussion at the end of the reading would be inappropriate, it provides a good opportunity to deal with questions, pose a few tactical ones in anticipation of the printed ones that follow and perhaps discuss relevant aspects of the text and illustrations. When the children are comfortable with the passage, it can be helpful if the text is "put back together again" by being read a second time.

The teacher may then wish to read through the questions with the children and alert them to particular requirements. Children must be encouraged to pay close attention to the exact wording of the question, and to consider it in its entirety before attempting an answer.

As their confidence grows, children will be happy working together in pairs and in groups, reading the passage and questions themselves. Teachers will need to be on hand to support, guide and focus attention when appropriate. Collaborative activities can be very supportive when the members are well matched and each contributes thoughtfully, but teachers need to be vigilant to spot those who are taking without giving, and simply copying the answers down.

Multiple choice activities lend themselves easily to consensus decisions, and can be self-marked by the group from the answers given in the Teachers' Handbook. The self-marking can be a learning activity too if the group returns to the text to establish the validity of the given answer where the group had made the wrong decision. Units where answers have to be given in the pupils' own words are sometimes less satisfactory as collaborative activities unless the children are sophisticated enough to benefit from the discussion and are happy to express themselves on paper independently. Pupils will find it more difficult to assess their own answers here by comparison with the suggested answers because wording may vary considerably.

The Teachers' Handbook allocates two pages to each Unit, and provides suggested answers and extension activities. Teachers may wish to give children a photocopy of the relevant pages and allow children to check their own work alongside the suggested answers, and then go on to work on the extension activities provided on the same sheets.

Key Comprehension can be used to give children an opportunity to work in controlled conditions from time to time in preparation for the National Curriculum Reading Comprehension tests (England and Wales, Northern Ireland) and 5-14 National Tests (Scotland). Children unused to working on their own and in silence can be disadvantaged and unnecessarily stressed during such unfamiliar formal tests. Units from Key Comprehension can be used for individual silent practice, and pupils can become accustomed to the rules of "no conferring" and "no asking questions". They can also become familiar with working against the clock if the practice is timed.

Lastly, the Units form a useful basis for homework assignments, where parental involvement can be guided and encouraged.

Reading comprehension terminology

Reading strategies

Skimming, scanning and detailed reading are essential strategies for effective information retrieval and to encourage full understanding and exploration of texts. All three strategies are developed during the course of Key Comprehension Book 4.

Skimming and scanning are terms much in use since the advent of the National Curricula. They are often used rather vaguely but are, in fact, two distinct reading strategies.

Skimming

Skimming involves reading swiftly through text in order to register the general outline (the gist) and omitting the detail. This gives the reader an overview of the material and an idea of where in the text, roughly, to find passages for closer reading later.

Scanning

Scanning involves rapid but focused reading of text in order to locate specific information, for example looking for particular details such as dates, names, certain types of words, and so on.

Detailed reading

Detailed reading involves reading text slowly and accurately in order to reflect upon the structure, purpose, content and tone of the text. The reader reads attentively, listening carefully to what the writer is saying.

When tackling the twenty-three Units in Book 4, pupils will have to employ skimming, scanning and detailed reading techniques on a regular basis. The questions direct pupils back to the text in order to find the answers. Pupils need to be told that referring back to the text is expected *(and is not cheating!)*. Reading Comprehension is not a memory test but an exercise in information retrieval and understanding.

Comprehension skills: literal, deductive, inferential and evaluative understanding

Key Comprehension Book 4 develops pupils' understanding of what they have read at several levels. As would be expected for upper juniors, the questions in the Units require deductive, inferential and evaluative understanding as well as literal understanding. These questions are designed to encourage pupils to read between the lines and interpret what they have read. A wide variety of questions is used to elicit a full range of responses requiring all these types of understanding.

Literal

Literal responses demonstrate the ability to understand the surface meaning of a text and to select information accurately from the text in answer to a question.
For example:

Question:	How did Roald Dahl first hear about the discovery of the treasure in Mildenhall? (Unit 4)
Answer:	*He read about the discovery in a newspaper.*

Deductive

Deductive responses demonstrate the ability to reach a logical conclusion by drawing on personal experience from beyond the immediate context of the passage.
For example:

Question:	In what ways did the bruise on the little boy's forehead resemble a poppy? (Unit 22)
Answer:	*The bruise resembled a poppy in three different ways: in size, colour and shape.*

Inferential

Inferential responses demonstrate the ability to reach a logical conclusion on the basis of information given.
For example:

Question:	Why do you think Mr Winslow is phoning the Royal Naval College? (Unit 8)
Answer:	*He is going to defend his son's honour and condemn the way the College has handled the affair.*

Evaluative

Evaluative responses demonstrate the ability to appraise, to form judgements and to weigh the evidence and its implications.
For example:

Question:	Can you guess what Tim does now that he knows the highwayman's plans? (Unit 15)
Answer:	*(A personal response is required here.)*

Range of question forms

The following chart summarises the range of question forms used in each Unit of work in Key Comprehension Book 4.

	true/false	multiple choice	answering in own words
UNIT 1		•	•
UNIT 2			•
UNIT 3	•	•	•
UNIT 4			•
UNIT 5			•
UNIT 6	•		•
UNIT 7			•
UNIT 8			•
UNIT 9		•	•
UNIT 10		•	
UNIT 11		•	•
UNIT 12	•		•
UNIT 13			•
UNIT 14	•		•
UNIT 15			•
UNIT 16			•
UNIT 17			•
UNIT 18			•
UNIT 19	•		•
UNIT 20			•
UNIT 21		•	•
UNIT 22			•
UNIT 23			•

Teaching comprehension skills

The National Curricula, and good teaching practice, enshrine the belief that comprehension skills can be taught.

To develop as effective readers, pupils should be taught to:
– read accurately, fluently and with understanding;
– understand and respond to the texts they read.
(*English in the National Curriculum, England and Wales, general requirements for English, p.2*)

The importance of meaning should be stressed at all stages. The activity of reading should take place, wherever possible, in an appropriate context, and it should be concerned with the gaining of meaning from a suitable text.
(*English Language 5-14, introduction to Reading Programme of Study, p.36*)

Pupils should develop the ability to read, understand and engage with various types of text for enjoyment and learning.
(*Revised Northern Ireland Curriculum, Reading Activities, p.8*)

So how can such relatively sophisticated skills be taught and developed?
What exactly can the teacher in the classroom do?

It is helpful to realise that understanding a text and answering accurately questions based on it involve a cluster of acquired skills:
1 detailed reading
2 search reading (skimming and scanning)
3 retrieval (identification and selection)
4 communication (speaking/writing)

Let us look more closely at each of these.

1 Development of detailed reading skills

Detailed reading (without skipping) gives the reader a clear grasp of the narrative. It enables the reader to know what the text is about, although more than one reading may be necessary to unlock the meaning fully.

Children can be helped to develop their detailed reading skills by answering questions, both orally and on paper, as teachers have long known. In the early stages a great deal of reading through the passages in the Units with the pupils may well be necessary. Dialogue and discussion, reading and talking about what is being read, help to focus a child's attention on the meaning of the words he or she may well have been reading fluently but without engagement. Children can be prompted by a supportive teacher to return to the text just read to find the right answer to a question. Such questioning and this textual referral help to encourage focused, attentive and reflective reading. It will also be useful to return to the text after the written answers have been completed to establish why some answers were incorrect or incomplete.

Detailed reading of the text is the key to understanding it. Needless to say, detailed reading of the questions is also very important.

2 Development of search reading skills (skimming and scanning)

When a child has an overview of a text, search reading skills are needed to locate quickly information required to answer a question. The child will know that the information is there somewhere but will need to be able to read through quickly to find it (skimming) and scrutinise when found (scanning).

The ability to skim over the surface of a text in search of information is a skill that children will probably not develop for themselves without encouragement. Many children, even at secondary level, have only one reading speed when tackling printed text.

Children can be encouraged to skim familiar texts by having small-group or whole-class *skimming races*. The teacher poses challenges such as "Find the place where it says in the passage that David has blue eyes". Winners have to put a finger on the right place in the text. It is wise to allow several children to raise their other hand triumphantly but then to intervene and show the rest before embarking on another search.

Scanning races yield information as well as location. The challenge above would be re-phrased as "Find the place in the passage where it tells us what colour David's eyes are". Winners would have to be able to locate the place in the text and retrieve the information. Children who simply remember the information get no credit here! The exercise is to locate the information with maximum speed.

3 Development of retrieval skills

The questions in the Key Comprehension series have been carefully devised to test (in a variety of forms) literal, deductive, inferential, and evaluative understanding.

Questions testing *literal* understanding will simply require children to retrieve the relevant information from the text. The clues will be lying on the surface of the text. Once children have become used to referring back to the text for the information they need (and not relying on memory alone or making up fanciful answers), this type of question should present no great difficulties. Children should enjoy locating and retrieving the answer.

Retrieving implicit meaning by *deduction or inference* is much more difficult, and children need to be helped to read between the lines. Questions targeting implicit meaning will be phrased along these lines: "How do you know that Sarah is the eldest child in the family?"; "Why do you think Tom feels so sad?" Children will be helped by gentle support here as they look for hidden clues. It does help to think of deductive and inferential retrieval skills as detective work! Plenty of practice is offered in Key Comprehension and children will gain much by working in pairs and small groups and exchanging their ideas as they discuss the text. Such discussions can be monitored by the teacher who can steer them away from unprofitable avenues and aim them in the right direction with some judicious questions. If children later have access to the answers in the Teachers' Handbook, they can see for themselves points in the given answers that they may have overlooked.

Increasingly in Book 4, *evaluative* answers are invited, requiring children to express an opinion which must be supported by close reference to the textual evidence. Such questions are open-ended and all pupils will have something valid to say. More able pupils will have the opportunity to marshal a cogent argument and to develop a view.

Children will meet a wide variety of question forms in the Units and it can be helpful to alert them to the demands each form presents. Earlier books in the Key Comprehension series include cloze, sequencing and sentence completion activities, but these are less relevant to the more demanding texts in Book 4.

Children should be warned that *true/false* activities may well lay traps for the unwary reader. Slight but significant variations of wording may render one choice unacceptable although very close to the truth. Children can be warned not to fall into the trap.

Multiple choice. Here again, distracters may well be included that are very nearly the answer required. Great vigilance is necessary and all the possible choices should be considered carefully before a decision is made. It can be helpful to eliminate any obviously incorrect statements and then to concentrate on choosing the right answer from the statements that remain.

When children are *answering in their own words*, they should be reminded not to lift material straight from the passage but to answer the question clearly in their own way. Sometimes there is more than one point to be made. Children should make sure they have included all that is relevant in their answer.

4 Developing communication skills

Whether children discuss a reading comprehension or write their answers in carefully controlled conditions, they are developing communication skills. In pair work and in small group discussions, ideas should be shared courteously and productively, and the quality of the reading comprehension shown can be assessed by the monitoring teacher.

Answering reading comprehension questions by writing the answers can be a very challenging exercise for children with limited writing skills. It is for this reason that a variety of approaches is used to familiarise them with the kinds of structures useful when they come to answer questions in their own words.

Reading comprehension is traditionally tested by the writing of answers to questions. The development of writing skills will be encouraged not only by answering the questions in each Unit but also by attempting the many extension activities in the Teachers' Handbook.

Teaching reading comprehension skills is an on-going classroom activity not, of course, confined to the English lesson. Such skills are vital if our children are to be enabled as enthusiastic, independent and reflective readers, as we would wish each one of them to be.

Key Comprehension and the National Curricula

Key Comprehension and National Curricula tests

Teachers may wish to use Key Comprehension Units formally in the classroom as preparation for National Curriculum Reading Comprehension tests (England and Wales, Northern Ireland) and 5-14 National Tests (Scotland).

Key Comprehension is a flexible resource and the Units may usefully be worked on in controlled conditions as children become more confident about working individually and independently of teacher intervention. For some children who are used only to working in pairs or groups, the experience of formally conducted tests can be a frightening one. Timed activities or conventions forbidding them to ask for help can be unfamiliar and bewildering.

Key Comprehension offers the opportunity of controlled practice in a supportive environment where the experience can be talked through beforehand and discussed afterwards. The overall task will gradually become familiar and the conventions understood. Children will be better prepared for formal tests if they have been given the opportunity from time to time of writing and working independently and quietly.

National Curriculum for England and Wales

The Key Stage 2 Programme of Study indicates three main areas of importance in Reading. These areas are: Range of reading, Key skills and Standard English and Language study. Key Comprehension is directed at nurturing skills of reading a range of texts with fluency, accuracy and understanding, and thus provides support for the Curriculum.

The following chart draws on key phrases and concepts from the Reading Programme of Study for Key Stage 2, as set out in *English in the National Curriculum* (HMSO 1995).

PROGRAMME OF STUDY REFERENCE	KEY COMPREHENSION BOOK 4
Range of reading **1a** Pupils should be encouraged to develop as enthusiastic, independent and reflective readers. Their reading should be developed through the use of progressively more challenging and demanding texts.	Texts chosen are interesting and motivating. Texts progress gradually in difficulty. Some texts are written for an adult audience.
1c Pupils' reading should include texts: with challenging subject matter; with complex structures; that include figurative language; with a variety of structural features.	Texts include a variety of styles, structures and genres; activities include questions which focus specifically on language and style.
1d The literature read should include: modern fiction, established fiction, poetry, texts from a variety of cultures, myths and legends.	Texts include recent, established and traditional children's fiction, adult fiction, poems, drama, information texts and transactional material.
Key skills **2b** Pupils should be taught to consider in detail the quality and depth of what they have read. They should be taught to use inference and deduction. They should be taught to evaluate the texts they have read and refer to relevant passages to support their opinions.	Activities target reading texts for understanding; comprehension questions require literal, deductive, inferential and evaluative responses; questions require pupils to refer back to the text to identify and retrieve information.
2c Pupils should be given opportunities to read for different purposes, using skimming and scanning to obtain specific information.	Activities require pupils to use skimming and scanning techniques to find information needed to answer questions.
Standard English and Language Study Pupils should be introduced to the features of different types of text. They should be encouraged to develop their understanding of the structure, vocabulary and grammar of Standard of English.	Texts include a variety of styles, structures and genres. Comprehension questions ask for answers written in complete sentences to encourage development of appropriate Standard English writing in a formal context.

English Language 5-14 Curriculum (Scotland)

Key Comprehension encourages children to read for meaning and with understanding and thus supports the 5-14 Curriculum.

The following chart draws on key phrases and concepts from the reading Attainment Targets of the Programmes of Study for Levels D-E, as set out in *English Language 5-14* (1991).

PROGRAMME OF STUDY REFERENCE	KEY COMPREHENSION BOOK 4
AT Strand **Reading to reflect on the writer's ideas and craft**	
Level D Read a variety of straightforward texts, and in discussion and writing show that they understand the gist of the text, its main ideas and/or feelings and can obtain particular information.	Extension activities in the Teachers' Handbook offer suggestions for follow-up work including discussion ideas and open-ended activities. Notes in the Teachers' Handbook identify the types of understanding tested by each question.
Level E Read independently, skim and scan, make predictions, identify subsidiary ideas, comment on author's style and attitudes.	The more challenging texts in Key Comprehension 4 involve all of these skills.
(Introduction to PoS) Learning to read accurately and with discrimination becomes increasingly important as pupils move through their education. The importance of meaning should be stressed at all stages. As texts become more complex and various in form, the teacher needs to deploy a widening range of techniques such as prediction, evaluating the text, making deductions, marking text, comparing and contrasting different texts.	Key Comprehension activities focus on developing reading with understanding.
Reading activities should demand that pupils show an overall grasp of a text, an understanding of specific details and how they contribute to the whole, make inferences, supply supporting evidence.	A variety of comprehension question forms and techniques is used. These include true/false, multiple choice and answering in own words, literal, inferential, deductive and evaluative question forms.
In teaching reading through all stages, in ways appropriate to pupils' age and attainment, the teacher can focus on texts: *before reading,* by priming pupils for the task, for example by alerting them to unfamiliar content or ideas; by directing them into the task;	Questions require pupils to read closely and use skimming and scanning techniques to retrieve specific information. Texts increase in difficulty gradually. The Teachers' Handbook suggests ways of introducing the formal comprehension activities, how to encourage the children to tackle the tasks and how to follow up the work.
during and after reading, by providing questions which ask for literal, inferential and evaluative responses; by asking them to demonstrate understanding by doing or speaking; by asking readers to use the text as a model for their own writing.	Activities include literal, inferential and evaluative questions designed to develop comprehension skills.

Northern Ireland Curriculum for English

The Northern Ireland Curriculum states that: "Pupils should develop the ability to read, understand and engage with various types of text for enjoyment and learning." (Programme of Study: Reading).

Key Comprehension supports this aim by targeting reading for understanding using a wide range of texts and question types.

The following chart draws on key phrases and concepts from the Reading Programme of Study for Key Stage 2 as set out in the *Northern Ireland Curriculum English* document (1996).

PROGRAMME OF STUDY REFERENCE	KEY COMPREHENSION BOOK 4
Reading Activities **a** listening to and understanding a range of texts	Understanding of a range of interesting and enjoyable texts is tested through a structured comprehension programme.
b/c participating in shared reading experiences; exploring stories and other texts with the teacher	The Pupils' Book lends itself to a range of classroom applications, from formal comprehension through to varied extension ideas in the Teachers' Handbook, including discussion points and open-ended activities.
f discussing and interpreting texts they have read **i** justifying their responses logically, by inference, deduction and reference to evidence within the text	Questions requiring literal, deductive, inferential and evaluative responses are included. Question types are fully referenced in the Teachers' Handbook.
l reconsidering their initial response to texts in the light of insight and information which emerge subsequently from their reading	Questions require pupils to locate specific details in texts, to interpret what they have read and to demonstrate their understanding. Evaluative questions and extension activities prompt a personal response.

Class record sheet

This sheet can be used to give an overall picture of the marks gained in each Unit by every pupil in the class.

READING COMPREHENSION

CLASS: YEAR: TEACHER:

UNITS (EACH MARKED OUT OF 15)

PUPILS' NAMES	1	2	3	4	5	6	7	8	9	10	11	12	13	14	15	16	17	18	19	20	21	22	23

Pupil record sheet

This sheet can be used to record in detail each pupil's performance in reading comprehension. The questions set in each Unit are arranged to highlight the type of reading comprehension tested. Question numbers appear in the top part of each rectangle leaving space in the lower part to indicate that each question has been attempted by the pupil. The right-hand column provides space to record the total mark out of 15 gained in each Unit.

READING COMPREHENSION

NAME: CLASS: YEAR:

UNIT	LITERAL	DEDUCTIVE	INFERENTIAL	EVALUATIVE	MARK	DATE
1	2, 3	1, 4, 5	6, 7, 8, 9	10		
2	1, 8, 12	3, 4, 6, 7	2, 5, 9, 10, 11			
3	1, 3, 6, 7, 8, 10	9	2, 4, 5			
4	1, 2, 6, 10	3, 4, 7, 8, 9	5			
5	5	2	1, 3, 6	4, 7, 8, 9, 10		
6	2, 9	3	1, 6, 7	4, 5, 8		
7	3, 4	2, 5, 6, 7, 10	1, 8	9		
8		10	1, 2, 3, 4, 7, 9	5, 6, 8		
9	1, 2, 3, 4, 5, 6, 7, 8	10	9			
10	1, 3, 10	7	2, 4, 5, 6, 8, 9			
11	3, 6	1, 2	4, 5	7, 8, 9, 10		
12	3, 9, 10	2, 4, 6, 8, 11	1, 5, 7, 12	13		
13	4, 5, 6, 7	1, 10	2, 3, 8	9		
14		3, 4, 8, 9	2, 6, 7	1, 5, 10		
15	5, 9, 12	4, 7	1, 2, 6, 8	3, 10, 11, 13		
16	1, 2, 3, 6, 7	4, 5, 8		9, 10		
17	1, 2, 4, 8, 10	3, 5	6, 7, 9			
18	5	3, 4, 10	1, 2, 6, 8	7, 9		
19	1, 6, 8, 9	10	2, 3, 4, 5, 7a	7b		
20	3, 4, 6	9, 10	1, 2, 5, 8	7		
21	8	3, 5	1, 4, 6, 7	2, 9, 10		
22	8	1, 2, 3, 4, 5, 6, 7, 9		10		
23	1, 3, 9, 10	2, 4, 5, 6, 7	8			

Bibliography

The texts used in Key Comprehension Book 4 are taken from the following sources:

Recent and established fiction

The Granny Project, Anne Fine, Methuen (Unit 2)
Jane Eyre, Charlotte Brontë, Penguin (Unit 10)
The Friends, Rosa Guy, Penguin (Unit 13)
Twist of Gold, Michael Morpurgo, Mammoth (Unit 16)
Goodnight Mister Tom, Michelle Magorian, Puffin (Unit 18)
The Village by the Sea, Anita Desai, Penguin (Unit 20)
The Legend of King Arthur, Andrew Davies, Armada (Unit 21)
Moonwind, Louise Lawrence, Bodley Head (Unit 23)

Poems

"The outing" by Michael Rosen, from *The Hypnotiser*, Scholastic (Unit 5)
"Tell me about your dream" by Gareth Owen, from *Another Fourth Poetry Book*,
    ed. John Foster, Oxford University Press (Unit 11)
"The highwayman" by Alfred Noyes, from *The New Dragon Book of Verse,*
    ed. Michael Harrison and Christopher Stuart-Clark, Oxford University Press (Unit 15)
"Mid-term break" by Seamus Heaney, from *The Puffin Book of Twentieth-Century*
    Children's Verse, ed. Brian Patten, Penguin (Unit 22)

Plays

The Winslow Boy, Terence Rattigan, Nick Hern Books (Unit 8)

Other prose

"Pinecones" by Robert Swindells, from *Autobiography*, ed. John Foster,
    Oxford University Press (Unit 1)
"A note about the next story" by Roald Dahl from *The Wonderful Story of Henry Sugar,*
    Puffin (Unit 4)
The Diary of Anne Frank, by Anne Frank, Longman (Unit 6)
"The wishes of Savitri" retold by Anthony Horowitz, from *The Kingfisher Book of Myths*
    and Legends, Kingfisher Books (Unit 7)
"Romeo meets Juliet" from *Shakespeare Stories* retold by Leon Garfield,
    Gollancz Children's Paperbacks (Unit 12)
Poetry for You, by C. Day Lewis, Basil Blackwell (Unit 14)

Information texts

More Fun with Science, Terry Cash and Steve Parker, Kingfisher Books (Unit 3)
Focus on Salt, David Lambert, Wayland (Unit 9)
"Learn to read or get lost" (adapted leaflet), Scottish Mountain Safety Group (Unit 17)
"Homework's coming home", John O' Leary, adapted from *The Times*, 20 January 1997
    (Unit 19)

PART TWO

Answers, mark scheme and extension activities

Answers follow for each Unit of Key Comprehension Book 4, together with a suggested mark scheme and suggestions for extension activities. Teachers may wish to photocopy relevant pages to allow pupils to mark their own work from the answers provided and to work on the extension activities suggested.

Answers

The activities often remind pupils to answer in full sentences in order to develop good practice from the outset. The answers suggested in the Teachers' Handbook are therefore supplied in full sentences where appropriate. In some places, open-ended questions invite a variety of possible answers and where this is the case, guidance is given on the kinds of response that are acceptable.

Mark scheme

The suggested mark scheme marks each Unit out of 15 to allow for some flexibility of response. Teachers may choose to award the suggested marks for accuracy of reading comprehension alone; or they may wish to reserve a part of each allocated mark for spelling, punctuation and sentence construction (for example, whether answers are written in full sentences). A photocopiable whole class record sheet is provided on page 14 and an individual pupil record sheet on page 15.

Extension activities

The extension activities offer opportunities for further work in reading comprehension, language work and writing in a wide range of genres. The specific skills covered are summarised at the end of each set of extension activities.

GENRE	autobiography
READING STRATEGIES	skimming; scanning; detailed reading
QUESTION FORM	answering in own words; multiple choice
UNDERSTANDING TESTED	questions 2, 3 – literal; questions 1, 4, 5 – deductive; questions 6, 7, 8, 9 – inferential; question 10 – evaluative

1 Explain what is meant by "first all-walking autumn" in paragraph four.
*Autumn 1943 is the first autumn in Robert's life when he is expected
to walk all the way and not ride part of the way in the pushchair.
(He is a big boy now!)* *(1 mark)*

2 List four different facts that we are told about the country cottage where the Swindells lived.
Accept four from the following list:
i) It was lit by gaslight.   *iv) The kitchen had a stone floor.*
ii) It had no piped (or running) water.   *v) It was two miles from the nearest town.*
iii) It had a big kitchen. *(2 marks)*

3 Why had Mrs Swindells and her two sons moved to the cottage in 1941?
*They had moved to the cottage to avoid the bombing in Bradford.
(They were less likely to be bombed in the country than they were in the town.)* *(1 mark)*

4 Which word in paragraph six indicates, as Robert Swindells says, that Mum
was "a fast walker"?
The word "strode" indicates that Mum was a fast walker. *(1 mark)*

5 How might the picture of the squanderbug have helped to stop people from
wasting food during the Second World War? Give all the good reasons you
can think of.
Accept any three:
*i) The swastika on the squanderbug's body would identify it with the enemy.
(The squanderbugs would be Nazis.)*
*ii) Nobody would want to be accused of helping to make the squanderbugs
fat by not using food carefully.*
*iii) Avoiding waste would be part of the "war effort" and a sign of patriotism.
Wasting food would be like treason.*
*iv) The imaginary insect, the squanderbug, would have a powerful image
and stay in people's minds.* *(3 marks)*

6 Why did Robert hesitate before picking up the pinecone in paragraph six?
*b) It might have been a bomb. (There had been rumours that the Germans
were dropping enticing little bombs to lure children into picking them up and
thus setting them off.)* *(1 mark)*

7 Why did Robert have to hold on to the pushchair for the rest of the journey?
*c) His mother was anxious about their safety and didn't want to linger.
(She recognised the danger that other German aeroplanes might fly over them
and the next time a bomb might be dropped.)* *(1 mark)*

8 What evidence is there in the passage to suggest that Robert was usually an
obedient child? *Accept any two:*
*i) He hesitated before picking up the pinecone and remembered that he was
not supposed to pick up unfamiliar objects (and why).*
*ii) He took shelter by the side of the road and stood still, as he had been taught
and without prompting, when he thought he heard the motorbike approaching.*
*iii) He obeyed his mother without complaint when he held on to the pushchair
for the rest of the journey.*
*iv) He kept running to catch up with his mother before the air-raid danger
and even when engrossed by the pinecones he knew how far his mother was
ahead of him. His mother never had to call him.* *(2 marks)*

9 Which word from the list below best describes Robert's mother? Explain your choice by referring to an incident in the passage as evidence. (Use a dictionary to check meanings if you wish.)
b) protective
Mrs Swindells behaved very protectively towards her children when the German aeroplane passed overhead. She rushed to get Robert and protected both children by covering them with her body. She acted very swiftly and without hesitation.   *(1 mark)*

10 Give two reasons why "Pinecones" is a good title for this true-life account.
"Pinecones" is a good title for these reasons:
i) It was while Robert was gathering pinecones for the first time in his life that the German aeroplane passed overhead.
ii) It was while he was playing with the pinecones the next day that he realised the Germans were "just people", something which he learned from the conversation between his mother and a neighbour.
iii) The title "Pinecones" reflects Robert's conclusion that pinecones are a lot more exciting than Germans if Germans are "just people" and not weird, menacing insects. He associates his discovery that Germans are human beings with finding his first pinecones.   *(2 marks)*

Extension activities

Research questions

Use reference books to help you find the answers to these questions.

1 Name a book written by Robert Swindells.

2 In what English county is Bradford?

3 When did the Second World War begin?

4 When did the Second World War end?

5 Name three different types of conifer tree that produce cones.

Writing

1 Imagine you are Robert's mother. Describe how you felt and what you did when you realised there was a German aeroplane overhead.

2 Interview a neighbour or a relation who grew up during the war and write an account of your interview.

3 Describe something that happened to you when you were very small that you still remember clearly.

NOW READ ON

If you enjoyed reading this true-life account of a childhood experience, you might enjoy the collection from which it comes: *Autobiography*, edited by John Foster.

SPECIFIC SKILLS   research and retrieval; autobiographical writing; writing in character; writing up an interview

The granny project

GENRE	children's fiction
READING STRATEGIES	skimming; scanning; detailed reading
QUESTION FORM	answering in own words
UNDERSTANDING TESTED	questions 1, 8, 12 – literal; questions 3, 4, 6, 7 – deductive; questions 2, 5, 9, 10, 11 – inferential

1 In what ways was the doctor "having a hard time" with the Harris family?
The doctor was finding it difficult to complete the form in the middle of such chaos and uproar. (1.5 marks)

2 Why did the doctor visit the Harris family if no one was ill? Was it a social visit?
No, it was not a social visit. He came to complete a form that was needed if Mrs Harris senior was to be accepted into a residential home. (2 marks)

3 Explain in your own words what was making the plates wobble so much.
The plates were defective. Something went wrong with the firing in the kiln which made them slightly lop-sided so that they didn't sit flat on the table. (1 mark)

4 Why was the doctor keeping "his head well down"?
The doctor was anxious to keep out of the imminent argument between husband and wife. (1 mark)

5 What made the doctor feel that Natasha Dolgorova was behaving like "a cool exotic childless woman"?
"Childless" because she was so detached from the chaos of the children's meal. She gave the impression that she didn't have any connection with the children at all. "Cool" refers to this lack of involvement in tone and action. "Exotic" because she was very beautiful (and very Russian) and seemed out of place in the kitchen. (1.5 marks)

6 We are told that Natasha Dolgorova was a Russian who had "defected to the West". What does this mean?
"Defected" means that she left her own country (Russia) to join an enemy country. The West (including Britain) and the former Soviet Union (including Russia) were enemies during the Cold War. (1 mark)

7 In what ways are Natasha's proverbs correctly described as "ominous", judging from the example here?
The proverbs are described correctly as "ominous" because they are gloomy, pessimistic and harsh. (1 mark)

8 Why did Sophie find newspapers useful for her Social Science projects?
Sophie found newspapers useful for these projects because they feature all the topics (crime, violence, police corruption, consumer protection, race relations, suicide and sex) that she would need to write about. (1 mark)

9 What is the relevance here of the Russian proverb, "You can't hide sharp steel spikes in soft cloth bags"?
Natasha meant that evasive answers and reassuring soft talk wouldn't hide the harsh truth that the grandmother needed residential care. The harsh truth is represented by the "sharp steel spikes" and evasion by the "soft cloth bags". (2 marks)

10 Find two words (not used together) that show Henry Harris was embarrassed at having to admit to his children that he was planning to move their grandmother into a residential home.
The two words that reveal his embarrassment are the verb "blushed" (when he had to admit it for the first time) and the adverb "uncomfortably" (when he tried to pretend that nothing had definitely been decided). (1 mark)

11 What made Natasha shoot the doctor "a venomous look" at one point?
Natasha was outraged by his comment that the old lady didn't present an immediate problem. As far as she was concerned, the old lady did!　　　*(1 mark)*

12 Do you find any evidence in the passage that the grandmother was behaving strangely? Explain.
She behaved oddly when she ate geranium leaves and feathers. She also stole Henry's slippers even though they were much too big for her.　　　*(1 mark)*

Extension activities

Additional questions

1 The children thought that their parents were heartless in wanting to send their grandmother to a residential home. What problems might they have been overlooking?

2 Explain the meaning of "uncensored description".

3 Cite two instances where Tanya exaggerated the truth.

4 Compare Henry's attitude to the problem of looking after his ageing mother with his wife's attitude.

5 How do you think the children's Granny Project could have been used to make their parents change their minds? Do you think the plan was likely to succeed?

Language

1 Two of Natasha's proverbs in the book are translated like this:
"The further into a wood you go, the more trees you find."
"Love is not a potato; you cannot throw it out of the window."
What are the wise points about life being made in these two proverbs?

2 Make a list of as many English proverbs as you can. (There are at least a hundred!)
Here are some less well-known ones to start you off:
"Shoemakers' wives are the worst shod."
"We never miss the water till the well runs dry."

3 You may like to start a collection of proverbs from other languages. Here's an Irish one:
"When best the fun, when best give over."

Writing

1 Write a description of an elderly person you know well. What makes him or her a really interesting person to visit?

2 "Children need grandparents!" Do you agree? Try to explain why the relationship between a grandchild and a grandparent is a very special one. Draw on your own experience.

NOW READ ON

Read *The Granny Project* to see how successful the children were in keeping their grandmother out of a home.

SPECIFIC SKILLS　additional questions; work with proverbs; descriptive writing; reflective writing

Battery power

GENRE	information text
READING STRATEGIES	skimming; scanning; detailed reading
QUESTION FORM	answering in own words; true/false; multiple choice
UNDERSTANDING TESTED	questions 1, 3, 6, 7, 8, 10 – literal; question 9 – deductive; questions 2, 4, 5 – inferential

1 What is used in batteries today instead of salt water?
A chemical paste is used instead of salt water. (1 mark)

2 Why did Volta need to put lots of "sandwiches" together when he made the first battery?
He put the "sandwiches" together to make the electrical current stronger. (1 mark)

3 Write out the statements that are true:
The true statements are:
a) The inventor of the first battery was an Italian scientist.
d) You need two different metals in a Voltaic pile.
e) Your tongue completes the circuit in the lemon experiment. (3 marks)

4 If you make your own Voltaic pile (according to the instructions "Make your own battery"), which metal will end up at the bottom of the pile, and which at the top?
Zinc will be at the bottom and copper at the top. (1 mark)

5 In the lemon experiment, why do you have to make sure that the two metals are not touching inside the lemon?
For the electricity to flow from one metal to another it must pass through the acid of the lemon juice. If the two metals touched, nothing would happen. (1 mark)

6 What is used instead of silver or copper in a modern battery?
A carbon rod is used instead of silver or copper. (1 mark)

7 Explain why batteries "run out".
Batteries run out because eventually all the chemicals are used up. (2 marks)

8 Why is salt water not used in modern batteries?
c) It would easily leak out. (1 mark)

9 Why is it highly dangerous to experiment with mains electricity or large batteries?
It is highly dangerous because the voltage is so powerful you could be killed. (2 marks)

10 Which electrical term has been named after Alessandro Volta and what does it mean?
The term "volt" has been named after him. A "volt" is a unit of measurement when calculating the power of an electrical current. (2 marks)

Extension activities

Research

1 Write a description of the types of batteries that are used today, and explain what they are used for.

2 You now know that the word "volt" is named after Alessandro Volta. Who gave their names to these words?
a) sandwich
d) cardigan
b) amp
e) wellingtons
c) watt

Writing

1 Give clear instructions for any other interesting experiment you know.

2 Write a story in which a flat battery plays an important part in what happens.

Language

1 In the passage the word "sandwich" was used both as a verb (doing word) and as a noun (naming word):

"<u>Sandwich</u> a piece of the salty blotting paper between a coin and a piece of zinc." (verb)

"He made a <u>sandwich</u> of paper soaked in salt water between a piece of silver and a piece of zinc." (noun)

Devise two sentences of your own for each word below, showing its use first as a verb and then as a noun:

a) base   d) tape

b) cut   e) touch

c) join

2 What is the difference in meaning between the words in these pairs of homophones (words that sound alike but are spelt differently)?

a) currant/current   d) bare/bear

b) way/weigh   e) place/plaice

c) one/won

3 How many meanings can you find for these words?

a) lead   d) pad

b) hide   e) lap

c) post

4 What is the difference in meaning between the words in these pairs? Use a dictionary, if you wish.

a) discover/invent   d) hope/expect

b) teach/learn   e) partake/participate

c) imply/infer

NOW READ ON

Find and read more information about batteries and electricity and write about their many different uses.

SPECIFIC SKILLS   research and retrieval; giving instructions; writing a narrative from given data; language – verbs and nouns, homophones, homonyms, verbs often confused

UNIT 4

A note about the next story

GENRE	autobiographical/personal
READING STRATEGIES	skimming; scanning; detailed reading
QUESTION FORM	answering in own words
UNDERSTANDING TESTED	questions 1, 2, 6, 10 – literal; questions 3, 4, 7, 8, 9 – deductive; question 5 – inferential

1 How did Roald Dahl first hear about the discovery of the treasure in Mildenhall?
He read about the discovery in a newspaper. *(1 mark)*

2 What actions tell us that he was extremely excited at the news of the discovery?
Accept these four:
i) He leapt from his chair.
ii) He didn't finish his breakfast.
iii) He shouted goodbye and rushed out to his car.
iv) He drove straight to Mildenhall. *(2 marks)*

3 Why do you think Gordon Butcher never wanted to see another reporter in his life?
He had obviously been pestered by reporters, all wanting the story for their newspaper.
He said that he had "had enough" of reporters. *(1 mark)*

4 Which words reveal that it took some time to persuade Gordon Butcher to tell Roald Dahl his story?
The words "in the end" suggest that it took some time. *(1 mark)*

5 Why do you think Gordon Butcher changed his mind and confided in Roald Dahl?
Accept two of these answers:
i) It could have been the offer of money by Roald Dahl if his story was published, although Gordon Butcher seemed very surprised when the cheque arrived later.
ii) Roald Dahl was not a reporter – Gordon Butcher may have thought that a short story writer sounded less threatening. He might also have been pleased that Roald Dahl was interested in his story.
iii) Roald Dahl promised to write a truthful story. Perhaps that persuaded Gordon Butcher – the newspapers might have misrepresented the story one way or another, and he saw Roald Dahl's story as a means of putting the record straight. *(2 marks)*

6 What further research did Roald Dahl do?
He attempted to hear Mr Ford's side of the story but Mr Ford wouldn't speak to him. (Those who have read the story will know why!) He also went to the British Museum (which had acquired the Mildenhall Treasure) to see the Roman silver for himself. *(1 mark)*

7 Why do you think Roald Dahl sent the story to the editor of an American magazine rather than a British one?
(Be generous here. It's a difficult question.) He chose an American rather than a British magazine because everyone in Britain would have read about the story already in the newspapers or heard about it on the radio. It would not be known in America. An American publisher would therefore be more likely to publish it than a British one. *(1 mark)*

8 Explain what Gordon Butcher meant when he said, "You could have knocked me over with a feather".
The expression means that he was taken completely by surprise. *(1 mark)*

9 Give the meaning of these words as used in the passage:
a) fair (first paragraph): *quite good/quite adequate*
b) remarkable (second paragraph): *noteworthy/very valuable/significant*
c) enthralling (fifth paragraph from end): *totally absorbing/quite spellbinding/fascinating*
d) superfluous (last paragraph): *not needed/surplus to requirements/unnecessary because the meaning was already clear* *(4 marks)*

10 When Roald Dahl came to revise the story for publication in book form some thirty years later, what kind of changes did he make?

He made small changes only, removing any sentences and any describing words which weren't really needed. He also rewrote some wordy passages more simply. *(1 mark)*

Extension activities

Additional questions

1 Do you think it helps a reader to enjoy a story more if background material like this passage is known?

2 Why do you think Roald Dahl wanted to meet Mr Butcher and Mr Ford before writing the story? Couldn't he have relied on the newspaper article?

3 What evidence is there in the passage to suggest that Gordon Butcher did not write many letters?

4 How did Roald Dahl feel when Mr Ford refused to tell him anything?

5 Do you think Roald Dahl was generous in giving Gordon Butcher half the money he earned from the publication of the story? Explain your answer.

6 The story itself tells us why the discovery of the Mildenhall treasure was kept secret for four years. If you have read the story, give the reason. If you have not read the story, suggest a possible reason.

Writing

1 Write the conversation that might have taken place between Gordon Butcher and his wife on the morning that Roald Dahl's cheque arrived.

2 How much do you learn about Roald Dahl as a writer and as a man from reading "A note about the next story"?

3 Write a newspaper article entitled: "Children discover buried treasure". Use lots of convincing details about the children's names, ages and addresses and describe whatever it is they found and how they found it. Include some comments by the children themselves, their parents and any experts you feel you want to call upon. Include photographs if you wish. Make the article look and sound like a newspaper article.

Vocabulary

1 "You could have knocked me over with a feather," wrote Gordon Butcher to describe how astonished he was to receive the cheque from Roald Dahl. What is the meaning of the following figurative expressions?
a) "She didn't bat an eyelid."   d) "They've let the cat out of the bag."
b) "You've hit the nail on the head."   e) "I'm only pulling your leg."
c) "I'm going to turn over a new leaf."

NOW READ ON

Read "The Mildenhall Treasure" to find out the information Roald Dahl obtained from Gordon Butcher.

SPECIFIC SKILLS additional comprehension questions; writing a conversation in character; extending the story; reflective writing; writing a newspaper article; imaginative writing; figurative expressions

The outing

GENRE	poem
READING STRATEGIES	skimming; scanning; detailed reading
QUESTION FORM	answering in own words
UNDERSTANDING TESTED	question 5 – literal; question 2 – deductive; questions 1, 3, 6 – inferential; questions 4, 7, 8, 9, 10 – evaluative

1 What three points about behaviour during the outing is the teacher trying to get across?
The three points are:
i) No eating or drinking before lunch at 12.15.
ii) Everyone must wait at the station to be told which train to get on.
iii) No screaming, racing about or sliding on floors at the museum. (1.5 marks)

2 Why is the second line of the poem in block capitals?
The second line is in capitals to show that the teacher is speaking more emphatically/loudly. (1 mark)

3 How can you tell that the teacher is finding it difficult to control the class?
Accept any four of the following:
i) The large number of incomplete sentences as the teacher constantly has to stop to address individual pupils.
ii) The frequent repetition of information shows that many class members are inattentive.
iii) There is plenty of evidence of bad behaviour: Mark does something dreadful; Phanh opens a can of drink; Mervyn shows off his sandwiches; Zoe interrupts; and so on.
iv) The sarcastic, negative tone suggests that the teacher feels stressed and more concerned with class control than enthusing about the visit to the museum.
v) The reference to appalling behaviour on a previous outing suggests that the teacher has little authority over the class. (2 marks)

4 How does Michael Rosen succeed in making the speaker here sound just like a certain type of teacher?
Accept any four sensible points, such as:
i) He captures the right bossy tone: "Right, class six".
ii) He uses certain recognisable expressions: "and that includes you".
iii) He uses names effectively.
iv) There is interaction with the class.
v) We recognise the heavy sarcasm: "You're in class six as well, aren't you?"
vi) We recognise the threats: "Any more, and you'll be out." (4 marks)

5 Why does the teacher say to Mervyn "Thank you, Mervyn, that's enough"? Enough of what?
(Be flexible here.) Most possibly it was Mervyn's flaunting of his jam sandwiches that evoked this outburst, but it is just possible that Mervyn was mimicking the teacher's thrice-repeated "No, we don't"! (0.5 marks)

6 What question did John ask the teacher?
We can assume that John asked the teacher what kind of ducks would be given Mervyn's jam sandwiches. (0.5 marks)

7 Which adjectives from this list accurately describe the teacher in the poem?
Two adjectives describe the teacher: sarcastic and harassed. (1 mark)

8 Do you think the pupils will behave well on the outing? Give your reasons.
Accept any well-reasoned answer. Most pupils will be pessimistic about the possibility of good behaviour, based on the children's past behaviour described in the poem, and their behaviour while the teacher is talking, as well as their lack of respect. (1 mark)

9 Do you like the last line of the poem as an ending or do you think it would be better to finish the poem a line earlier? Why?
Accept any well-reasoned and well-supported answer. Some pupils will feel the poem should end with the note of finality ("we're off!"), but more perceptive pupils will appreciate the despairing tone of the existing last line and the sort of day it suggests! (1.5 marks)

10 Did you enjoy reading this poem? Give your reasons as clearly as you can.
Accept sensitive, well-reasoned responses here. Reasons for enjoying the poem might include: humour; a recognisable situation; accessibility; language; technique (the teacher is speaking but there are implicit pupil contributions). (2 marks)

Extension activities

Additional questions

1 What is the response of the class to their teacher? Base your answer on a close study of the poem.

2 Make a list of all the pupils mentioned by the teacher and what we know about them.

3 What do you think Mark did (verse four)?

4 What advice would you give to the teacher in this poem after hearing the way he or she speaks to the class?

Writing

1 Describe a school outing you have particularly enjoyed and make it clear exactly what made it so enjoyable.

2 If you were a teacher, what rules would you insist that a class observe on an outing?

NOW READ ON

Find more poems by Michael Rosen in your class or school library, and in the public library.

SPECIFIC SKILLS   additional comprehension questions; personal writing; reflective writing

Anne Frank's diary: 1942

GENRE	diary
READING STRATEGIES	skimming; scanning; detailed reading
QUESTION FORM	answering in own words; true/false
UNDERSTANDING TESTED	questions 2, 9 – literal; question 3 – deductive; questions 1, 6, 7 – inferential; questions 4, 5, 8 – evaluative

1 On what date did the Franks go into hiding?
The Franks went into hiding on Monday, 6 July 1942.   (1 mark)

2 At what time did they leave home?
They left home at 7.30 am.   (1 mark)

3 Why was it "lucky" that it was cooler than the day before?
It was lucky that it was cooler because everyone was wearing several layers of clothes.   (1 mark)

4 Why do you think that Anne had deliberately not been told where the hiding place was?
She was not told for reasons of security. What she did not know she could not reveal accidentally or under pressure. (The lives of those hiding there could depend on Anne's ignorance if she were to be captured on the way to the hiding place. The lives of their helpers were also at risk.)   (1 mark)

5 Anne was just thirteen years old when she wrote these extracts (her diary was given to her as a birthday present on 12 June). What evidence is there in the passage to suggest that she was younger than Margot?
Accept any two thoughtful points. Pupils may comment that:
i) Margot, who was sixteen years old, had been "called up", while Anne hadn't, which suggests she was younger.
ii) If Anne were seventeen or older, her parents might have treated her rather differently. She is excluded from adult discussions.
iii) Margot took control in her parents' absence when Anne wanted to answer the door. This suggests the action of an older sister.
iv) The general tone of the diary entries sounds young – that of a teenager at the lower end of the age range.   (2 marks)

6 True or false? Write out the statements that are true.
The true statements are:
b) Anne called their hiding place "The Secret Annexe".
d) The Franks and Van Daans planned to share the same hiding place.
e) Anne was the only member of the Frank family who liked hearing the Westertoren clock.   (3 marks)

7 According to Anne, no Jew in the same situation as her family would dream of going out with a suitcase full of clothes. Why not? Explain why this would have been a dangerous thing to do.
It would have attracted attention, suggesting that those concerned were planning to leave the area. (Jewish people were not free to move around as they wished.)   (1 mark)

8 Look at the belongings that Anne packed in the satchel. She calls these some of her most "vital" possessions. What do they tell us about Anne as a person?
Accept any three thoughtful points. Pupils will probably suggest:
i) Anne cared about her appearance (shown by the hair curlers and comb).
ii) The diary was very important to her; she needed to confide in it as a friend.
iii) She was serious about study and wanted to keep up with school work when she was hiding (the school books are evidence of this).
iv) She valued memories, as is shown by her wish to keep old letters.   (3 marks)

9 In what ways was Anne finding it difficult to adjust to being in hiding?
Anne mentions three areas of particular difficulty. Accept any two of these:
i) She didn't like the oppressive silence in the evening and at night.
ii) She found it very difficult to have to stay indoors all the time.
iii) She felt very vulnerable to discovery.   *(2 marks)*

Extension activities

Additional questions

1 Why do you think Anne Frank wrote her diary entries as if they were letters to a friend? What advantage does this give?

2 In what ways was the Secret Annexe an "ideal hiding place"?

3 Anne describes being in the Secret Annexe as "like being on holiday in a very peculiar boarding house". Explain why.

4 Write a full description of Anne as a person using all the evidence provided in these extracts.

5 Would you like to read more of *Anne Frank's Diary*? Give reasons for your response.

Writing

1 Anne says that her world had been turned upside-down. If you had to go into hiding with your family, what aspects of your present life would you miss most? What aspects of being in hiding do you think you would find most difficult?

2 Write two diary entries in the style of Anne Frank, recording the events of yesterday and today.

3 Write Margot's diary entry for Wednesday, 8 July 1942, giving her view of the events that Anne writes about.

4 Some people think that Anne Frank's diary is private and should not have been published after her death. What do you think?

5 Have you ever kept a diary? Write from your own experience about some of the pleasures and some of the difficulties involved.

Language

1 Compose sentences showing that you know how each of the words in the pairs below should be correctly used:
   a) quiet and quite   d) where and were
   b) diary and dairy   e) does and dose
   c) clothes and cloths

NOW READ ON

Read more of Anne Frank's diary and find out what happened to her.

SPECIFIC SKILLS   additional comprehension questions; personal writing; reflective writing; diary writing; writing a diary in character; spelling

The wishes of Savitri

GENRE	sacred story from Hindu scriptures
READING STRATEGIES	skimming; scanning; detailed reading
QUESTION FORM	answering in own words
UNDERSTANDING TESTED	questions 3, 4 – literal; questions 2, 5, 6, 7, 10 – deductive; questions 1, 8 – inferential; question 9 – evaluative

1 How did destiny find a husband for Savitri?
Destiny brought her to the forest and prompted her to question the tall, handsome man. (1.5 marks)

2 What is the meaning of "declined" (paragraph two)?
"Declined" means "refused politely". (1 mark)

3 Why was everyone at home dismayed to hear that it was Satyavan whom Savitri wanted to marry?
They were dismayed because they learned through Narada that Satyavan had been cursed. He had only four years to live. Savitri would be a widow for most of her life. (1 mark)

4 How long were Savitri and Satyavan married before the god of death came for him?
They were married for four years. (1 mark)

5 What is a noose and why did Yamaraja carry one?
A noose is a loop in a rope (as in a lasso) that tightens when the rope is pulled. Yamaraja released the souls from the bodies of the dying by placing the noose over their heads. (2 marks)

6 What was Yamaraja's reason for giving Savitri her first wish? (Use your own words.)
Yamaraja wanted to cheer her up a little, to lessen her sadness at her husband's death. (1 mark)

7 What was Yamaraja's reason for giving Savitri her second wish? (Again, use your own words to explain.)
Yamaraja gave Savitri her second wish partly because he admired her love for her husband, but partly in the hope that she would then go home. (2 marks)

8 How did Savitri's third wish save her husband's life?
It saved his life because Yamaraja granted Savitri's wish to have many children before he realised that Satyavan was the only man who could be their father. (Hindu widows do not remarry.) So to keep his word about the children, he had to restore their future father to life. (2 marks)

9 In what ways do you find Savitri a remarkable woman?
Accept any four sensible answers based on the text, possibly:
i) She was highly courageous in following the god of death almost to his kingdom.
ii) She was very clever to have used her three wishes so successfully. Her father-in-law got his sight back and his kingdom and riches, and her husband was restored to life.
iii) She was gentle but firm in refusing to let her father arrange a marriage for her at the age of eighteen. This would be very unusual at the time and she handled it well.
iv) She had strong principles and would not break her promise to marry Satyavan even when she knew about the dreadful curse.
v) She was willing to marry a poor man and live in poverty when she was a princess and could have enjoyed every luxury.
vi) Her faith was very profound. Few young women would have spent a year, as she did, talking to holy men, praying at shrines and living a life of such austerity. (2 marks)

10 What words or phrases could replace the underlined words below?
a) He was overthrown and underlined{banished}. – *exiled/sent away from his kingdom*
b) She had already underlined{plighted} herself to Satyavan. – *solemnly pledged*
c) "You and I must part company, underlined{lest} I decide to keep you in my shadowy kingdom for all eternity." – *in case* (1.5 marks)

Extension activities

Writing

1 Write a letter from Savitri to her father (begin "My dear father,"), telling him the wonderful news.

2 Describe a wedding you have attended, saying in what ways it was similar to Savitri's and in what ways it was different.

3 "Local Hero Saves Boy". Write an article for your local newspaper with this headline.

4 Savitri was granted three wishes. If you could have three wishes come true, what would you wish for?

5 Do you know anyone who has shown great courage? Write about the difficulties that had to be overcome.

Language

1 A prefix is a syllable (or syllables) added to the beginning of a word. By adding a prefix to these words from the passage, make them opposite in meaning:
   a) experience   d) faithful
   b) happiness   e) happy
   c) normal

2 Complete this table. The first example has been done for you.

Noun	Verb
a) occupation	occupy
b) devotion	–
c) grief	–
d) laughter	–
e) –	decide
f) –	conspire
g) –	suggest
h) –	discover

3 Complete this table. The first example has been done for

Noun	Adjective
a) curiosity	curious
b) instinct	–
c) nobility	–
d) roughness	–
e) –	certain
f) –	dutiful
g) –	angry
h) –	musical

NOW READ ON

Find and read another sacred story. Describe how the story is similar to or different from "The wishes of Savitri".

SPECIFIC SKILLS   retelling the story; writing a letter in character; descriptive writing; evaluative writing; writing a newspaper article; personal/reflective writing; negative prefixes; forming nouns, verbs and adjectives

The Winslow boy

GENRE	drama
READING STRATEGIES	skimming; scanning; detailed reading
QUESTION FORM	answering in own words
UNDERSTANDING TESTED	question 10 – deductive; questions 1, 2, 3, 4, 7, 9 – inferential; questions 5, 6, 8 – evaluative

1 Why is Desmond staring "gloomily" into his glass?
He is miserable at the news of Catherine's engagement because he wants to marry her himself. (1 mark)

2 Why is Arthur surprised to hear that Violet has brought a glass for Ronnie?
He is surprised because he thinks that Ronnie is miles away at the Royal Naval College. (1 mark)

3 Why has Ronnie been sent home before the end of term?
Ronnie has been sent home in disgrace because the College authorities believe he has stolen and cashed a postal order. He will not be allowed to return to the college. (1 mark)

4 Why is Mrs Winslow reluctant to read aloud the letter Ronnie has brought with him?
She doesn't want the two non-members of the family to hear the contents. She's particularly anxious that John should not know of the disgrace to the family. (1 mark)

5 Why do you think everyone is afraid of Mr Winslow?
Accept any sensible, well supported comments. These points may be made:
i) He is very much the head of the family (in charge and dominant).
ii) He speaks authoritatively ("Grace, what does this mean?" etc).
iii) He gives orders and expects them to be obeyed.
iv) He keeps his feelings to himself and this makes him seem more remote and unapproachable than he really is. (2 marks)

6 Catherine tells John earlier in the play that her father "worships" Ronnie. What evidence is there in this extract that Mr Winslow loves Ronnie very much?
Accept any four points:
i) He is very anxious when he thinks his son is ill and wants to be with him.
ii) He is gentle but firm when alone with his son.
iii) He is hurt that Ronnie is frightened of him.
iv) There is clearly a long-standing relationship. Mr Winslow told Ronnie a long time ago always to come to him first when in trouble.
v) He doesn't threaten Ronnie. He says he won't be angry.
vi) He is clearly going to defend his son when he phones the Royal Naval College. (2 marks)

7 How does Mr Winslow satisfy himself that Ronnie is telling the truth?
Accept any two points:
i) He asks him twice after reassuring Ronnie that all he wants is the truth.
ii) He looks Ronnie in the eye all the time so that he can judge whether his son is telling the truth.
iii) He assures Ronnie that he will detect a lie without a shadow of a doubt.
Ronnie passes this test and Mr Winslow is satisfied. (2 marks)

8 Who do you think is the more decisive character, Catherine or her mother? Give your reasons.
Catherine is the more decisive character. This is shown on several occasions (accept any two):
i) She "instinctively takes command" when Arthur questions his wife about Ronnie being at home. She sends Violet away.
ii) She speaks "steadily" when her father misunderstands the reason for Ronnie being sent home early and her father "realises the truth from the tone of her voice".
iii) Her mother turns to Catherine for advice and guidance when uncertain how to break the news of Ronnie's disgrace to her husband. Catherine confidently indicates that she should produce the letter and that she should read it aloud as asked.

*iv) She gives her strength by waiting for her mother at the door when the family leave
Arthur alone to wait for Ronnie.* *(2 marks)*

9 Why do you think Mr Winslow is phoning the Royal Naval College?
*He is going to defend his son's honour and condemn the way the College has handled
the affair.* *(1 mark)*

10 Suggest words or phrases that could replace the underlined words in these stage directions:
   a) VIOLET <u>lingers</u>, smiling – *dawdles/seems reluctant to leave*
   b) She <u>extends</u> her glass – *holds out*
   c) The others are frozen with <u>apprehension</u> – *dread of what will happen next*
   d) After an <u>appreciable</u> pause, there comes a timid knock – *considerable/quite long* *(2 marks)*

Extension activities

Writing

1 Write the scene where Violet goes down to the servants' room and tells her best friend
   about what's happening upstairs. Remember to read the extract again to check exactly
   how much Violet knows. She doesn't know the full story.

2 Read the extract again. It is written with a stage performance in mind. How much would
   be lost if it were performed on the radio?

Language

1 "Lunch" is the word used widely nowadays for the meal which Arthur Winslow calls
   "luncheon". What is the full form of these words now widely used in their shortened form:
   a) pram   f) bus
   b) flu   g) phone
   c) vet   h) perm
   d) zoo   i) chips
   e) disco   j) fridge

2 In the first stage direction, Terence Rattigan requires "a general buzz of conversation".
   "Buzz" is an example of onomatopoeia (the word itself sounds like the noise it names).
   Can you think of five other examples of onomatopoeia? It may help to think of the sound
   that dry leaves make underfoot, the sound of waves in a storm, the sound that cars make
   when they come to a sudden stop, and so on.

NOW READ ON

Read more of *The Winslow boy* and find out what happens to Ronnie.

SPECIFIC SKILLS   extending the story; writing in character; writing a scene of a play;
                  expressing and justifying a point of view; language work – contractions, onomatopoeia

Salt is special

GENRE	information text
READING STRATEGIES	skimming; scanning; detailed reading
QUESTION FORM	answering in own words; multiple choice
UNDERSTANDING TESTED	questions 1, 2, 3, 4, 5, 6, 7, 8 – literal; question 10 – deductive; question 9 – inferential

1 Where do we get our supplies of salt from today?
We get our supplies from two sources: from the sea and from underground mines.　　(1 mark)

2 How many tonnes of salt are consumed world-wide in a year?
Approximately 170 million tonnes are consumed world-wide in a year.　　(1 mark)

3 Mention three different uses of salt in food production.
Salt is used in food production:
i) To preserve food
ii) To flavour food
iii) To freeze (ice-cream)　　(3 marks)

4 List three (non-food) products used today that required salt at some stage of their manufacture.
Accept any three from: soap; toothpaste; soft water; clothes made from dyed fabrics; leathers and suedes; synthetic rubber; paper.　　(3 marks)

5 Why is salt used on icy roads?
Salt is used on icy roads to melt the ice and to prevent more forming.　　(1 mark)

6 What part does salt play in the treatment of some very sick patients?
Some very sick patients need to be fed by means of a saline drip. Liquid food mixed with a salt solution is passed slowly into a blood vessel.　　(1 mark)

7 Name two countries which once put a tax on salt.
Britain and France once put a tax on salt.　　(1 mark)

8 What is salt mainly used for today?
d) It is used in the manufacture of chemicals.　　(1 mark)

9 What is the connection between salt and our modern word "salary"?
Roman soldiers were paid partly in salt. They called this part of their wages their "salarium" (sal = salt in Latin). Our word "salary" comes from "salarium".　　(1 mark)

10 What do these words mean in the passage?
a) brine (paragraph four)
"Brine" is a solution made of very salty water.
b) adhesives (paragraph five)
"Adhesives" are substances used to stick things together.
c) synthetic (paragraph five)
"Synthetic" means artificially and not naturally produced.
d) deposed (paragraph ten)
"Deposed" means removed from power.　　(2 marks)

Extension activities

Additional questions

1 Explain exactly how the French salt tax (the *gabelle*) caused hardship to the poor.

2 Why was the *Via Saleria* built and where did it start and finish?

3 What part did salt play in the battle between the Romans and Carthaginians?

4 What simple test could you use to see whether your water at home is hard or soft?

5 Look at every paragraph in the passage and decide what topic each one is about.

Research

1 By referring to the Old Testament of the Bible, a good dictionary and other sources, find the answers to these questions.
   a) Who became a pillar of salt?
   b) What does SALT stand for?
   c) On what occasion would a superstitious person throw salt over his or her left shoulder?
   d) What is the derivation of "below the salt" and what does it mean?
   e) How would an "old salt" have earned his living?

Expressions

Salt has made its way into a lot of our everyday expressions. Use each of these in a separate sentence to show that you understand what it means:
a) to "rub salt into someone's wound"
b) to "take with a pinch of salt"
c) to be "the salt of the earth"
d) to be "worth one's salt"
e) to "put salt on someone's tail"

Language

1 What is the precise difference in meaning between these financial terms?
   a) salary
   b) wages
   c) bonus
   d) commission
   e) fee

NOW READ ON

Find and read some more examples of information texts. Use a table of "good points" and "bad points" to indicate how well you think the text explains the information.

SPECIFIC SKILLS   additional comprehension questions; research and retrieval; expressions (colloquialisms); paragraph topics; vocabulary

Jane Eyre

GENRE	adult fiction/literary classic
READING STRATEGIES	skimming; scanning; detailed reading
QUESTION FORM	multiple choice
UNDERSTANDING TESTED	questions 1, 3, 10 – literal; question 7 – deductive; questions 2, 4, 5, 6, 8, 9 – inferential

1 What made Jane ill?
   c) She had been locked in a dark room.   *(1.5 marks)*

2 Why didn't Jane live with her parents?
   b) Her parents were dead.   *(1.5 marks)*

3 What was Bessie's position in the household?
   d) She was the nursemaid.   *(1.5 marks)*

4 What was the surname of Jane's mother before she married?
   c) Reed   *(1.5 marks)*

5 What did Abbot mean when she described Jane as "a little toad"?
   a) She meant that Jane was ugly.   *(1.5 marks)*

6 Why was Mr Lloyd pleased when Bessie had to go to the servants' hall for dinner?
   b) He wanted to question Jane without being interrupted.   *(1.5 marks)*

7 Why did the friends and family of Jane's mother disapprove of the man she married?
   d) He was not rich enough.   *(1.5 marks)*

8 Why did Mr Lloyd think it might be a good idea for Jane to go away to school?
   b) He thought she should get away from Gateshead Hall.   *(1.5 marks)*

9 Why did Mr Lloyd want to see Mrs Reed before he went?
   a) He wanted to suggest that Jane went to school.   *(1.5 marks)*

10 Why did Bessie and Abbot feel sure that Mrs Reed would let Jane go away to school?
   a) They knew she would be glad to get Jane out of the house.   *(1.5 marks)*

Extension activities

Additional questions

1 How did Bessie's attitude to Jane differ from Abbot's?

2 Reading between the lines, what did Mr Lloyd think about Jane's situation at Gateshead Hall?

3 Make a list of all the reasons why Jane was unhappy.

4 Explain in your own words the meaning of the sentences:
   a) Punctuality at meals was rigidly enforced at Gateshead Hall.
   b) Her father cut her off without a shilling.

5 What evidence can you find in the passage to support the doctor's description of Gateshead Hall as "a very fine place to live in"?

Language

1 Suggest single words that could take the place of the underlined words:

a) "Oh! I dare say she was crying because she could not go out with the missis in the carriage," <u>interposed</u> Bessie.

b) "The fall did not make you ill; what did then?" <u>pursued</u> Mr Lloyd.

c) Children can feel, but they cannot <u>analyse</u> their feelings.

d) "Yes, I dote on Miss Georgiana!" cried the <u>fervent</u> Abbot.

2 Explain exactly why capital letters are used in the words and phrases listed below:

a) Gateshead Hall

b) John Reed

c) a Welsh rabbit

d) I

3 In sentences of your own, give six more examples of capital letters being used for other reasons than the four reasons in the last exercise.

Writing

1 Write the conversation that took place between Mr Lloyd and Mrs Reed.

2 Read the passage again, noting all the clues that tell you what kind of girl Jane was. Write a description of Jane at this point in her life.

3 Have you ever been unfairly punished for something you didn't do, or punished in a way you thought was cruel? Were your feelings about your punishment the same as Jane's or different? Explain.

4 What do you think of this extract? Was it hard to understand? (The book from which it comes was first published in 1847.)

NOW READ ON

Read more of *Jane Eyre* and find out what happens to her.

Tell me about your dream

GENRE	poem
READING STRATEGIES	skimming; scanning; detailed reading
QUESTION FORM	answering in own words; multiple choice
UNDERSTANDING TESTED	questions 3, 6 – literal; questions 1, 2 – deductive; questions 4, 5 – inferential; questions 7, 8, 9, 10 – evaluative

1 Who do you think is saying the words, "Tell me about your dream"?
c) a counsellor or therapist (There's a sense that the speaker is finding it therapeutic to talk, and that this is the purpose. The questioning is professionally skilled to make clear the confusion between fantasy and reality. The invitation to ask questions at the end confirms the choice of professional counsellor or therapist as interlocutor.)   *(1 mark)*

2 Why is only one volunteer needed if two players have missed the train?
Only one volunteer is needed as the reserve can play too.   *(1 mark)*

3 Why does the manager hold the dreamer back when the other players leave the dressing room?
He holds the dreamer back to tell him the news that he wants him to be captain. He also tells him that he wants him to be the last out of the tunnel so that he can be alone to enjoy all the cheers from the crowd.   *(1 mark)*

4 What makes the dream so frightening that the dreamer always wakes up "sweating with fright"?
Accept any two sensible points:
i) The dreamer is overwhelmed with panic at being so hopelessly lost.
ii) The dreamer feels deeply ashamed that he has let "his" team down.
iii) The dreamer feels he has disgraced himself publicly.
iv) The dreamer is conscious that time is racing by, and this adds to the stress.   *(2 marks)*

5 We can deduce that the speaker is asked a number of questions as he relates his dream. List four of the questions put to him.
Accept any four:
i) Do you remember what the voice says?
ii) So, in your dream, you don't know whether you are dreaming or not?
iii) What have you done about it?
iv) Has it helped you to talk about it?
v) Do you want to ask any questions?
Allow these other possible questions:
vi) Would you like to talk me through your dream?
vii) You're at a football match in your dream, aren't you?
viii) Do you have your boots with you?   *(2 marks)*

6 What steps has the speaker taken to ensure that this dream never becomes reality?
He no longer takes his boots with him to matches because then he can't volunteer to be a substitute player and the rest of the dream can't come true.   *(1 mark)*

7 How old do you think the speaker is? Give your reasons.
Those pupils who think that the speaker is a boy might cite the following reasons:
i) He is called "lad" by the manager.
ii) His dream is a common fantasy among young football fans.
iii) He must be young to surrender to the fantasy!
Those who think that the speaker is a grown man might cite:
i) The occasional adult turn-of-phrase ("never varies", "waiting for the teams to emerge")
ii) The adaptation of the listener's questions ("Do I remember what it says?" etc).
iii) He is tall enough for the manager to look him in the eye.
Others may combine these two sets of points and see the dreamer as an adolescent!   *(2 marks)*

8 Explain what fear lies behind the last line of the poem.
   The speaker is afraid that he may be dreaming this conversation. It is becoming hard
   to separate dreams from reality.   (1 mark)

9 How does Gareth Owen make the dream convincingly dreamlike? Give at least three points.
   These points may be made:
   i) The unlikelihood of the request for a volunteer (this could only happen in a dream).
   ii) The fantasy of being elevated to the captaincy.
   iii) The dream of having famous players shaking his hand and clapping him on the back.
   iv) The nightmare sequence of white corridors leading nowhere.
   v) The fact the dream recurs without any changes.
   vi) The details that stand out clearly and the vagueness of the rest ("suddenly I'm in the
   dressing room").
   vii) The uncertainty of whether it's a dream or not because it's so familiar.   (3 marks)

10 Why do you think this poem will appeal to a lot of readers whether they are interested
   in football or not?
   Accept any two thoughtful points, such as:
   i) It's a funny, amusing poem.
   ii) We recognise our own fantasies (perhaps in a slightly different context).
   iii) We identify with the nightmare sequences.
   iv) Our interest is held throughout the poem.
   v) There's a nice twist in the tale.   (1 mark)

Extension activities

Writing

1 Imagine that the speaker in the poem writes to the agony page of a magazine instead of
   consulting a therapist face-to-face. Write his letter and also the agony aunt's reply.

2 Do you have a dream which you've dreamed again and again? Is it pleasant or unpleasant?
   Describe your dream.

3 Write a story about a boy or a girl of your own age who achieves fame by stepping
   forward in an emergency.

4 We have concentrated on dreams and fantasies in this Unit so far. Let us end by returning
   to reality. What is your ambition in life and how do you plan to achieve it?

5 Do you think that fox-hunting, stag-hunting, otter-hunting and hare-coursing are sports?
   Would you ban them?

6 Write about your hobby, interest, or involvement in a sporting activity.

NOW READ ON

Use poetry anthologies to find and read more poems about hobbies and interests.
Which is your favourite, and why?

SPECIFIC SKILLS   recasting the story; writing a letter; descriptive writing; personal writing; writing a story;
                  reflective writing

Romeo meets Juliet

GENRE	narrative (prose retelling of a Shakespeare play)
READING STRATEGIES	skimming; scanning; detailed reading
QUESTION FORM	answering in own words; true/false
UNDERSTANDING TESTED	questions 3, 9, 10 – literal; questions 2, 4, 6, 8, 11 – deductive; questions 1, 5, 7, 12 – inferential; question 13 – evaluative

1 Explain how the brawling between the Capulets and the Montagues was "destructive".
It was destructive in three ways:
i) It disturbed the peace.
ii) It damaged property.
iii) It endangered innocent passers-by (as well as threatening Capulet and Montague lives). *(1.5 marks)*

2 In the first sentence, the men of Verona are described as being "as bright as wasps". Explain.
This could refer to the brightness of their colourful dress at that period. It could also refer to their liveliness, energy, bloodthirstiness, argumentative nature, and so on. *(1 mark)*

3 How did Benvolio get involved in the fighting?
He attempted to make peace between the two sides but then Tybalt started fighting him. *(1 mark)*

4 Explain in your own words the ultimatum the Prince issued to the Capulets and Montagues.
The Prince said that anyone causing trouble in the future would be put to death. *(1 mark)*

5 Write out the statements that are true.
The true statements are:
a) Romeo had no brothers.
b) Romeo lived in Verona.
c) Romeo and Benvolio were cousins. *(1.5 marks)*

6 Put these words spoken by Lady Montague into clear, modern English.
"O where is Romeo, saw you him today? Right glad I am he was not at this fray."
"Have you seen Romeo anywhere today? I wonder where he is. I'm really glad he wasn't involved in this brawl/fight/fracas." *(1 mark)*

7 Why did Benvolio suggest to Romeo's parents that they leave him alone with Romeo for a while?
He promised to find out what was bothering Romeo, but he needed to be alone with him to get him to talk. *(0.5 marks)*

8 Look at paragraph nine, beginning "The parents departed ...". Suggest words or phrases that could replace these:
a) departed – *left/went away*
b) gloom – *depression/melancholy/bad mood*
c) doted to distraction upon – *adored/was obsessed by/worshipped/was infatuated by*
d) consequently – *as a result/because of this/so* *(2 marks)*

9 How did Romeo find out that Rosalyne would be at the Capulets' banquet?
He found out by sheer luck. The Capulet servant who had been told to invite all the guests couldn't read very well and asked Romeo to read the guest list to him. Rosalyne's name was on the list. *(0.5 marks)*

10 Give two reasons why Romeo and his friends were masked and in fancy dress at the banquet.
It was the custom for uninvited guests to be masked and to wear fancy dress. In addition, it would have been very dangerous for any Montagues to be recognised in a Capulet house because the two families were enemies. *(1 mark)*

11 Romeo had a "premonition" before entering the Capulets' house and seeing Juliet for the first time. What is a "premonition"?
A premonition is a strong feeling that something unpleasant or tragic is going to happen, before it actually happens. (1 mark)

12 It seemed strange that the servant didn't know who Juliet was when Romeo questioned him. Can you think of a good reason to explain why he might not have known?
Accept any sensible reason. A possible explanation is that the servant was one of the many extra servants likely to be hired for the banquet, and would not have known the members of the family. (1 mark)

13 Benvolio is described as "a sensible Montague". In what ways did he appear sensible in this extract?
He showed himself to be sensible throughout the extract in these ways:
i) He attempted to break up the brawl.
ii) He knew how to handle Romeo.
iii) He suggested that the parents leave.
iv) He gave Romeo good advice. (2 marks)

Extension activities

Additional questions

1 Use an atlas to find out which country Verona is in.

2 What was the reaction of the ordinary citizens of Verona to the feuding between the Capulets and the Montagues?

3 There is a simile in the first sentence of the extract: "where men were as bright as wasps". Find three more similes in the extract. Say which you find the most vivid and why.

4 What is the meaning of the underlined words as used in the passage?
   a) some semblance of peace
   b) had incensed him beyond measure
   c) drifted dolefully into the square
   d) but Romeo was adamant

5 Use reference books to find out in which year *Romeo and Juliet* was first performed.

Writing

1 Imagine you are one of the mothers who had to drag their children out of the way of the brawling Montagues and Capulets that hot July morning. Write a letter to a friend, telling her all about it.

2 You are an ace reporter for the *Verona Echo* and you were on the spot when everything happened. You took down every word that the Prince said and you managed in addition to interview some of the citizens. Write your front-page news story for the next day's edition. Keep to all the facts as given but add any details you need to make your article vivid and convincing.

NOW READ ON

Read more of *Romeo and Juliet* (either the original play, or a retelling of the story) and find out what happens to the two leading characters.

SPECIFIC SKILLS   additional comprehension questions; research and retrieval; extending the story; writing in character; writing a letter; writing a newspaper article

GENRE	teenage fiction
READING STRATEGIES	skimming; scanning; detailed reading
QUESTION FORM	answering in own words
UNDERSTANDING TESTED	questions 4, 5, 6, 7 – literal; questions 1, 10 – deductive; questions 2, 3, 8 – inferential; question 9 – evaluative

1 "Al – all the chi – child – ren bunch up and wa – ant to fi – fight me." Why are Phyllisia's words printed in this broken-up way?
Accept any sensible answer but note that Phyllisia was not crying (the tears were "unshed").
Phyllisia's words are printed like this because:
i) She was nearly crying.
ii) Her lips were so swollen that she could hardly form the sounds.
iii) She was choked with nostalgia/homesickness for the West Indies. *(1 mark)*

2 What were her mother's feelings when Phyllisia told her she was being bullied?
Accept any two:
i) She was shocked.
ii) She felt sorry for her/sympathetic.
iii) She felt grave/serious/concerned. *(1 mark)*

3 Explain why hearing her mother's voice and accent made Phyllisia want to cry.
Hearing her mother's voice and accent reminded her of the West Indies where she came
from. She longed to go back there and away from this new, strange place. *(1 mark)*

4 Why were the girls bullying her, according to Phyllisia?
She thought they hated her because she answered the teacher's questions in class and
they considered her the teacher's pet. *(1 mark)*

5 Why were the girls bullying Phyllisia, according to her mother?
The were picking on her because she was the outsider. Her mother believed that once
the girls got to know Phyllisia, the bullying would stop. *(1 mark)*

6 What different forms was the bullying taking?
The bullying was taking various forms (accept any two):
i) Physical violence.
ii) Name-calling.
iii) Public criticism.
iv) Ambushing Phyllisia.
v) Mobbing her.
vi) Isolating her. *(1 mark)*

7 Why wouldn't her mother let her leave the school and go to another one?
Her mother said that she had to deal with the problem once and for all at this school.
Moving to another school would not solve the problem. She had to learn to fight it. *(2 marks)*

8 Give two reasons why Ruby deliberately said as little as possible in class.
Accept any two:
i) Ruby said very little so that she could pass unnoticed.
ii) She didn't want to alienate girls who were less intelligent than she was by showing
she was clever.
iii) She wanted to fit in with the attitudes of the group.
iv) She wanted to keep her West Indian accent as low-key as possible. *(1 mark)*

9 Was "being liked" equally important to both girls? Give reasons for your answer.
   Accept any sensitive answers here. Possibly:
   Ruby admitted she wanted to be liked. She wanted to be liked so much by her
   classmates that she sacrificed being praised by the teacher and she tried to suppress
   everything that would make her seem "different" from them.
   Phyllisia denied she wanted to be liked but was evidently deeply unhappy at being hated.(2 marks)

10 Suggest words or phrases which could take the place of the words underlined below:
   a) Ruby did not notice the <u>reproach</u> in Mother's voice. – *gentle criticism/rebuke*
   b) <u>Aghast</u>, Mother cried: "Is so? For shame, for shame, Ruby." – *horrified*
   c) <u>Stifling</u> the urge to throw myself on the floor, to kick, to scream, have a tantrum,
   I screeched instead, "But it's me they're fighting." – *smothering/suppressing*
   d) She smiled <u>condescendingly</u>. – *in a superior way/in a grand manner*   (*4 marks*)

Extension activities

Additional questions

1 What did Phyllisia mean when she said, "I don't bargain with my intelligence"?

2 Do you find Phyllisia's reaction to her experience of bullying convincing? Does the author,
  Rosa Guy, understand?

3 What did Phyllisia admire about her mother?

4 What do we learn about Ruby in this extract (appearance, attitudes, relationship with
  mother and sister, and so on)?

5 Do you think Phyllisia should have gone to school the next day? Give reasons for your
  answer.

Writing

1 What general advice would you give to anyone who is being bullied?

2 Bullying can take many forms. Making someone feel left out is a form of bullying as well
  as hitting and punching. What is the saddest case of bullying you have ever known?

3 It can be very lonely starting again at a new school and leaving friends behind. Write an
  actual (or imaginative) account of your first day at a new school.

NOW READ ON

Read more of *The Friends* and find out what happens to Phyllisia and her family.

Two ways of looking at a daffodil

GENRE	discursive prose
READING STRATEGIES	skimming; scanning; detailed reading
QUESTION FORM	answering in own words; true/false
UNDERSTANDING TESTED	questions 3, 4, 8, 9 – deductive; questions 2, 6, 7 – inferential;
	questions 1, 5, 10 – evaluative

1 Why does C. Day Lewis bother to mention the baby?
The example of the baby is important to his argument. Like the baby, the poet has to use all five senses to explore the surrounding world. Like the baby, the poet must retain a sense of excitement and curiosity. *(1 mark)*

2 Which senses is the baby using while exploring the mysterious orange?
Accept up to three senses. The baby is using:
i) Sight (staring at the orange).
ii) Smell (the orange has a strange smell).
iii) Touch (fingering the orange).
iv) Taste (dribbling on the orange).
(Hearing is not used, unless you argue that the baby drops the orange and listens to the result!) *(3 marks)*

3 What is a "sense of wonder"?
Accept any sensitive answer, for example it is the capacity to be moved, enchanted, delighted, astonished, intrigued, and so on. *(1 mark)*

4 In the poem referred to, the daffodils are described as "fluttering and dancing".
How can daffodils "flutter" and "dance"?
The movement of the daffodils in the breeze would stir the petals. They would look like the fluttering wings of yellow butterflies in that respect. The lively swaying of the stems and flower heads could be compared with people twirling and manoeuvring on the dance floor. *(1 mark)*

5 Which of the two descriptions of the wild daffodils do you prefer, or do you find them both equally interesting? Give your reasons as clearly as you can.
There are no "correct" answers here. Accept any well supported choice. Be especially generous to anyone who says both (on the grounds that they are written for different purposes). *(1 mark)*

6 True or false? Write the statements that are true.
The true statements are:
a) Scientists want to find out the facts.
c) Scientists investigate the world around them.
d) Scientists want to make connections between things. *(3 marks)*

7 In what ways can a poet "sharpen" our senses?
Accept any one point. A poet can sharpen our senses by:
i) Helping us to see the world through his or her eyes.
ii) Encouraging us to explore our own responses.
iii) Enriching our memories.
iv) Awakening our imagination as we read. *(1 mark)*

8 What is the meaning of "novelty"? (paragraph one)
"Novelty" here means the newness and unfamiliarity of everything. *(1 mark)*

9 What is meant by "peculiarities" in the last paragraph?
"Peculiarities" means "unique characteristics", "special habits", "funny ways". This is "peculiar" in the sense of "special" rather than "strange". *(2 marks)*

10 Do you think that "Two ways of looking at a daffodil" is a good title for this passage? Give reasons for your response.
Accept any well-reasoned answer. Possibly:
Yes:
i) The two approaches to describing a daffodil are explored at length.
ii) It's an interesting title and would make you want to read on.
No:
i) The writer is more interested in exploring the poetic approach and so the title suggests a balance that isn't there.
ii) The title is baffling until you read on. It would be better if it was more straightforward. (1 mark)

Extension activities

Additional questions

1 In the introduction to the book from which this passage is taken, C. Day Lewis writes: "What I do hope is that this book will help you to enjoy reading poetry, will persuade you that poetry is one of the great things of life which it would be a shame to miss ..." Analyse the way he is presenting his case in this extract by working out the topic of each paragraph and showing how one leads to the next.

2 List three famous poets and explain why you think they are famous.

3 Do the same for three famous scientists.

Writing

1 C. Day Lewis says it's very difficult indeed to describe what a friend is really like. Do your best to describe a special friend. Do you feel you have succeeded in your description?

2 Have you ever read a poem which made you see the world differently? Write about the poem and why you like it so much.

3 Copy out a poem you have written yourself and discuss how you came to choose that subject, what feelings you wanted to communicate, how difficult it was to write, what particularly pleases you about it now and what you would like to be able to improve if you could.

NOW READ ON

Find some more examples of scientific and poetic descriptions. Do they fit with the argument put forward by C. Day Lewis? Explain, with reference to the descriptions.

SPECIFIC SKILLS   paragraph topics; analysing an argument; research and retrieval; descriptive writing; analytical writing

UNIT 15   The highwayman

GENRE	poem
READING STRATEGIES	skimming; scanning; detailed reading
QUESTION FORM	answering in own words
UNDERSTANDING TESTED	questions 5, 9, 12 – literal; questions 4, 7 – deductive; questions 1, 2, 6, 8 – inferential; questions 3, 10, 11, 13 – evaluative

1 What makes the moon look like a "ghostly galleon"?
The moon is seen briefly appearing from banks of cloud in the dark sky. It looks like a pale ship ploughing its way through heavy seas. (1 mark)

2 Explain why "ribbon" is a good way of describing the road across the moor.
The road in the moonlight is seen stretching across the expanse of the moors. It looks like a long narrow ribbon. This comparison helps us to see the moonlit road clearly in our imagination. (1 mark)

3 Say these lines to yourself:
"And the highwayman came riding –
    Riding – riding –
The highwayman came riding, up to the old inn-door."
Do you like the repetition of "riding"? What does it suggest about the highwayman and his journey?
Accept any two points. The repetition effectively suggests:
The long distance the highwayman has to cover.
The speed and urgency of his pell-mell ride.
The galloping of his horse's hoofs. (1 mark)

4 Which word in verse two tells us that the night sky is full of stars?
The word "jewelled" tells us that the night sky is full of stars (shining brightly). (1 mark)

5 Find the two verbs in verse three which describe the noise made by the hoofs of the highwayman's horse when he rides into the inn-yard over the cobbles.
The two verbs are "clattered" and "clashed". (1 mark)

6 Why is Tim jealous?
Accept either:
i) Tim is jealous of the highwayman because he loves Bess too.
ii) He is jealous that Bess loves the highwayman and not him. (1 mark)

7 What colour is Tim's hair and how would it feel if it's like "mouldy hay"?
His hair is blond/dark blond/dirty blond. It would feel rough, damp and matted. (1 mark)

8 A "cascade" is a waterfall. How is Bess's hair just like a waterfall for a few seconds?
Bess has very long hair which has been tied up in a plait. She is at a first-floor window looking down on the highwayman below. When she lets her hair hang loose to its full extent it tumbles down (like a waterfall). (1 mark)

9 Why is the highwayman in a hurry and when does he promise to return?
The highwayman is in a hurry because he has work to do (robbing travellers).
He promises to return before the morning if possible, but certainly by the next night, whatever happens. (1 mark)

10 Can you guess what Tim does now that he knows the highwayman's plans?
Tim informs the authorities (King George's men) and they come to capture the highwayman. (1 mark)

11 Why is the highwayman called "the dead man" (in Part two, verse three) when he is not dead?
Accept any sensible answer. Pupils will not know the technical term "prolepsis" but may well see how effectively this anticipatory device is used here in warning us of the highwayman's fate and so making Bess's sacrifice doubly sad because it is in vain. (2 marks)

Key Comprehension Ginn & Co 1998. Copying permitted for purchasing school only. This material is not copyright fre

12 How does Bess try to save the highwayman from being captured by King George's men?
She fires the musket (which kills her) and hopes this warning shot will make him avoid the inn. (1 mark)

13 Do you think the poem has a happy or a sad ending? Give your reasons.
Accept any well-reasoned answers here.
i) Pupils favouring the ending as happy may suggest that the ghostly lovers are immortal, that the two died in the fullness of their love, that both died generously for the other's sake.
ii) Pupils favouring the ending as sad may suggest that any ending is sad when both characters die, that Bess sacrificed her life in vain, that the ghostly ending is sad because the lovers will never progress beyond courtship. (2 marks)

Extension activities

Additional questions

1 Show how the highwayman in this poem is made to seem an exciting and glamorous hero. (Think about the way he is dressed, his actions, and his words.)

2 Explain how highwaymen "earned" their living.

3 What does the highwayman in the poem mean when he says he's after "a prize" that night?

4 What weapons does the highwayman carry?

5 What do these words and phrases mean?

Part one

a) torrent (verse one)	d) peaked (verse four)
b) thigh (verse two)	e) harry (verse five)
c) shutters (verse three)	f) casement (verse six)

Part two

g) sniggering jest (verse three)	i) drenched (verse eight)
h) spurred (verse eight)	j) brandished (verse nine)

6 There are lots of sounds in this poem. Make a list of all the sounds you can find.

7 There are lots of colours mentioned. Make a list of all the colours and what they describe.

Writing

1 Imagine that you are Tim, the ostler. What do you do when the highwayman rides off? How do you feel? Continue the story.

2 Re-tell the first part of the story from Bess's point of view. What were you doing when the highwayman arrived in Part one? How long have you known him? How do you feel about him?

NOW READ ON

If you enjoyed this poem, you might like to read other poems that tell a story. Find and read "The Listeners" by Walter de la Mare; "Flannan Isle" by W.W. Gibson; "The Lady of Shalott" by Alfred, Lord Tennyson.

SPECIFIC SKILLS additional questions; writing in character; extending the story; retelling the story

Twist of gold

GENRE	children's fiction
READING STRATEGIES	skimming; scanning; detailed reading
QUESTION FORM	answering in own words
UNDERSTANDING TESTED	questions 1, 2, 3, 6, 7 – literal; questions 4, 5, 8 – deductive; questions 9, 10 – evaluative

1 How did the Dragoon feel about being hated by Irish children?
He always felt hurt. (1 mark)

2 Who had told the boy to have nothing to do with soldiers?
His mother had told him to have nothing to do with them. (1 mark)

3 How could the Dragoon tell that the boy was starving and close to death?
There were all the physical signs that the boy was starving (sunken eyes, sunken cheeks, thin legs and bony knees), but it was the desperate way the boy was fishing for food that finally brought it home to him. (2 marks)

4 The Dragoon was "exhilarated" when the boy spoke to him at last.
a) What does "exhilarated" mean?
"Exhilarated" means overjoyed.
b) What does this reaction tell us about the Dragoon?
This reaction shows how much the Dragoon cared about helping the boy. (2 marks)

5 Suggest words which could take the place of the underlined words in the sentences below.
a) The man sensed the boy's burning enmity. – *hatred/hostility*
b) He had encountered it often enough before. – *met*
c) The truth dawned on him in all its clarity. – *clearness/fullness* (3 marks)

6 What was the Dragoon's first name?
The Dragoon's first name was Will (William). (0.5 marks)

7 What was the boy's first name?
The boy's first name was Sean. (0.5 marks)

8 Explain in your own words the underlined parts of these sentences.
a) It was a close still evening and the flies were down.
The flies had arrived and were flying above the surface of the water.
b) The boy baited his hook.
The boy fixed his bait (a worm perhaps) to the hook on the end of his fishing line in order to tempt a fish to bite it.
c) The Dragoon's horse stood with his legs in the cool of the water and drank tidily.
The horse drank without too much splashing or disturbing the surface of the water. (3 marks)

9 What do you feel is especially significant in the boy and the Dragoon meeting mid-way across the river?
They each travelled an equal distance and each made an equal effort. (1 mark)

10 What does the boy's body language tell us about what he was feeling when the biscuits were given to him? (He held them tightly; he smelt them; he didn't take his eyes off them.)
Accept any two:
i) His body language tells us how precious the biscuits were to him.
ii) He could hardly believe his good fortune.
iii) He could hardly believe it was happening to him.
iv) He wanted to check that it was real and not a dream. (1 mark)

Extension activities

Additional questions

1 Explain the Dragoon's comment to himself: "You're looking at a dead child."

2 Why did the Dragoon keep addressing Sean as "son"?

3 Which sentence tells us that the Dragoon had seen Irish children even thinner than Sean?

4 What was it about the Dragoon's voice that convinced Sean he was not going to hurt him?

5 Do you think the boy was wise to trust a stranger?

Writing

1 Imagine that you are William, the Dragoon Sergeant. Write a letter home to your family in England telling them all about your meeting with Sean O'Brien.

2 Write the conversation that could have taken place between Sean and his mother (and his little sister, Annie, who is not mentioned in this passage) when he returned home with the biscuits.

3 The Dragoon was a kind man who hated the suffering he saw all around him in Ireland, and yet the Irish saw him automatically as an enemy because he was an outsider. They jumped to conclusions about him. Write a story that shows how important it is not to jump to conclusions.

Language

Complete this table. The first example has been done for you.

Adjective	Noun
cool	coolness
skeletal	–
–	impulse
exhilarated	–
–	clarity
still	–
–	humanity

NOW READ ON

If you would like to find out how the Dragoon helped the O'Brien family, read the rest of *Twist of Gold* by Michael Morpurgo.

SPECIFIC SKILLS   additional comprehension questions; extending the story; writing a letter in character; writing dialogue in character; work with nouns and adjectives

Learn to read or get lost

GENRE	information leaflet
READING STRATEGIES	skimming; scanning; detailed reading
QUESTION FORM	answering in own words
UNDERSTANDING TESTED	questions 1, 2, 4, 8, 10 – literal; questions 3, 5 – deductive; questions 6, 7, 9 – inferential

1 What two things do you need to be able to read to avoid getting lost on the Scottish hills or mountains?
You need to be able to read a map and a compass. *(2 marks)*

2 Why is it a good idea to plan two routes before you go walking or climbing?
It is a good idea to plan two routes (the route you hope to take and an alternative) in case of problems, such as the weather making the first route impossible. *(1 mark)*

3 Why should you always tell a responsible person where you are going?
You should always tell a responsible person where you are going so that a search can be made for you in the right area if you don't return on time. *(1 mark)*

4 Why is it so difficult to calculate in advance how long a walk will take in the Scottish hills and mountains? Give as many reasons as you can.
The walk will take longer than planned:
i) If you have to zig-zag your way up a slope instead of walking straight up.
ii) If you have to pick your way slowly over difficult land instead of marching across.
iii) If poor weather conditions slow you down.
iv) If you have to go a longer way around some parts of the route because they have become impassable. *(4 marks)*

5 Which word in the first section (Introduction) means "stretches of rock fragments on steeply sloping ground"?
The word is "scree". *(1 mark)*

6 Why is it a good idea to seek local advice?
It is a good idea because people who live in the area and know the hills and mountains really well can tell you things no map can. *(1 mark)*

7 Why should you always study a map of the area carefully before you set off?
(Accept any two of the responses below.) You should study a map of the area carefully, so that:
i) You can plan two routes accurately.
ii) You can calculate approximately how long the walk will take.
iii) You know in advance what the difficulties are likely to be. *(1 mark)*

8 Why should you take a map with you when you go walking or climbing?
You should take a map with you to help you stay on course, and to help you work out where you are if you get lost. *(2 marks)*

9 Why do you need to take a compass with you?
A compass will help you to stay on course, even in poor visibility. *(1 mark)*

10 What are you advised to do if you get completely lost?
If you get completely lost, you should use your compass to work out the safest way home. *(1 mark)*

Extension activities

Additional questions

1 What is the meaning of:
   a) impassable   c) selected
   b) terrain   d) navigation

2 What information is conveyed by the contour lines on an Ordnance Survey map?

3 What is the difference between conditions "deteriorating" and "becoming worse than expected"?

4 What is the advantage of zig-zagging up a steep slope?

5 What particular problems in conditions of poor visibility do summits and meetings of ridges present?

6 How does the time the walk will take depend on the fitness of the weakest member of the group?

Writing

1 What would you say to someone who said that planning a long walk in advance takes all the fun out of it?

2 Write a review of the Scottish Mountain Safety Group's leaflet. Consider content, presentation and suitability for the target audience.

3 "Lost on the mountain": write a story about a group of young climbers who lose their way while climbing a steep mountain. You can choose whether to have sensible climbers who had planned everything they could in advance, or foolish climbers who set off without planning anything.

4 Have you ever been lost? Perhaps as a small child you were separated from an adult for a short time in a shopping centre or somewhere else. Did you panic? Describe how you felt.

5 Design a poster for the Scottish Mountain Safety Group to reinforce their message.

6 Devise your own "Key Points to Remember" to help younger pupils tackle comprehension questions more effectively.

Language

1 What is the difference between:
   a) affect and effect   d) advice and advise
   b) alternate and alternative   e) route and rout
   c) phase and phrase

NOW READ ON

Find and read some more public information leaflets that advise on safety (especially on holiday). Decide what is good and bad about the leaflets – for example, is all the information presented clearly?

SPECIFIC SKILLS   additional comprehension questions; expressing and defending a point of view; writing a critical review; writing a fictional narrative; personal writing; devising a poster; vocabulary

Meeting

GENRE	children's fiction
READING STRATEGIES	skimming; scanning; detailed reading
QUESTION FORM	answering in own words
UNDERSTANDING TESTED	question 5 – literal; questions 3, 4, 10 – deductive; questions 1, 2, 6, 8 – inferential; questions 7, 9 – evaluative

1 Why was the Billeting Officer "relieved" when Tom Oakley agreed to let Willie live with him?

Accept any two points. She was relieved because it made her burden lighter, and Willie's mother had been very specific about a foster home near a church or placement with a religious person. This limited possible "homes". Also:
i) Another child had been placed so she could get on with her job.
ii) She might have thought that an old man living alone would not want an evacuee – but he agreed to take Willie.
iii) She was overriding the house owner's right "to choose a child" but Tom didn't object. *(1 mark)*

2 Why was she wearing an armband?

The armband identified her as Billeting Officer. Tom looked at her armband. *(1 mark)*

3 Which word tells us that she was not finding her job of placing the children in foster homes an easy one?

The word "harassed" suggests that she was not finding it easy. *(1 mark)*

4 What did she mean when she said that the declaration of war was "imminent"?

She meant "about to happen". *(1 mark)*

5 In what ways was Tom Oakley's appearance the very opposite of Willie's?

Accept up to four contrasts:

Tom	Willie
i) brown	*complexion pale*
ii) healthy	*sickly-looking*
iii) thick white hair	*limp sandy hair*
iv) stockily built	*thin/bony elbows and knees*
v) average height	*small*
vi) well into his sixties	*very young (eight years old)*

(2 marks)

6 Why did Willie have so many bruises?

His mother beat him. (She told Willie they were "soft beatings" but they clearly had hurt him.) *(1 mark)*

7 What clues are there in the passage that show Tom was really a kind man although he sounded fierce?

Accept any four of the following points or examples:
i) Tom's second look at Willie (thin and sickly-looking, limp sandy hair and dull grey eyes) led to his agreeing (gruffly) to take him. His heart was touched by what he saw.
ii) He was considerate, shown by:
- His intention to put the peg at Willie's height.
- Cooking bacon for him and being generous with sugar (which was rationed).
- Heaping coke on the fire to keep Willie warm.
- Lending Willie a warm scarf.
iii) He was perceptive, for example:
- He noticed Willie's lack of appetite and didn't force him to eat.
- He noticed Willie's embarrassment when he asked about his bruise.
- He changed the subject when he saw Willie's distress.
- He avoided mentioning the bruise on Willie's thigh.
- He was reassuring about the graveyard. He anticipated the fear that Willie might have had. *(2 marks)*

8 Why was Willie so desperately anxious to "be good"?
He wanted to avoid being beaten. His mother said she beat him because he was "bad". He feared the beatings he thought Tom would give him because he looked stronger than his mother, so his beatings would hurt even more. (1 mark)

9 Write a paragraph on what you learn about Willie's background from this extract.
Reward generously any thoughtful and relevant points. Perhaps:
i) Willie came from a single-parent family.
ii) He was an only child.
iii) His mother was very strict and beat him.
iv) He was neglected, shown by his thin clothes and the fact that he was wearing plimsolls because he had no shoes.
v) He was underfed and very thin (he was not used to eating bacon).
vi) He was unloved – shown by his cowed, listless, timid manner.
vii) His mother seemed fanatically religious but very cruel. (3 marks)

10 What is the meaning of the underlined words?
  a) "His mother wants him to be with someone who's religious or near a church. She was quite <u>adamant.</u>"
  "Adamant" means unwilling to change her mind/unwilling to budge.
  b) He didn't feel at all hungry, but remembered <u>apprehensively</u> what his Mum had said about doing as he was told.
  "Apprehensively" means with fear and dread.
  c) Bacon was a luxury. Only <u>lodgers</u> or visitors had bacon and here he was not eating it.
  "Lodgers" are long-stay visitors in someone's house who pay for their room and meals.
  d) One of his socks slid half-way down his leg, revealing a large <u>multi-coloured</u> bruise on his shin.
  "Multi-coloured" means many-coloured. (2 marks)

Extension activities

Additional questions

1 How can you tell that the Billeting Officer for the area did not come from Tom's village?

2 What might Willie's thoughts have been as he watched the Billeting Officer go away?

3 Why exactly did Willie "pale" and "pull his sock up quickly" when Tom noticed his bruise and swollen red sore?

Writing

1 Imagine that Willie had been told by his mother to write her a letter before he went to bed the night he arrived. Write the letter.

2 Write about an occasion when you spent a night away from your family.

Language

1 The underlined words are adverbs – these words describe the way in which an action is done.
  i) "Yes," said Tom <u>bluntly</u>. ("Bluntly" describes "said".)
  ii) <u>Nervously</u>, Willie followed him. ("Nervously" describes "followed".)
  Find ten more adverbs in the passage and identify the words they describe.

NOW READ ON

Read more of *Goodnight Mister Tom* and find out what happens to Willie and Tom.

SPECIFIC SKILLS additional comprehension questions; writing a letter in character; personal writing; adverbs of manner (identification and function)

Homework's coming home

GENRE	newspaper article
READING STRATEGIES	skimming; scanning; detailed reading
QUESTION FORM	answering in own words; true/false
UNDERSTANDING TESTED	questions 1, 6, 8, 9 – literal; question 10 – deductive; questions 2, 3, 4, 5, 7a – inferential; question 7b – evaluative

1 Why has the Principal of King Edward VI Handsworth School for Girls reduced the amount of homework set to eleven- to thirteen-year-olds at her school?
She has reduced the amount of homework set to eleven- to thirteen-year-olds because she wants to allow more time for after-school and leisure activities. (1 mark)

2 Does Peter Miller at Smithfield High do more or less homework per week than the average British fourteen-year-old? Explain.
Peter does much more homework than the average fourteen-year-old. He does sixteen hours a week, whereas the average British fourteen-year-old does six hours a week. (1 mark)

3 Out of the four pupils interviewed:
a) Who enjoys doing homework the most?
Emily Smith enjoys doing homework the most (but she does the least, at two hours a week).
b) Who enjoys doing it the least?
Peter Miller enjoys doing it the least (but he does the most, at sixteen hours a week). (1 mark)

4 True or false? Write out the statements that are true.
The true statements are:
b) Dutch fourteen-year-old pupils have more homework on average than British fourteen-year-olds.
c) Girls are more likely than boys to spend hours and hours on their homework.
e) Teachers may expect homework to take a certain amount of time to do but some children will need more time and some less.
Note: the unwary may answer that (d) is true, but careful reading of the last sentence of the article will show that it's the hours spent doing homework (rather than homework itself) that seems not to correlate with improved exam results. (3 marks)

5 Why does Lucy Adams wish she had been given more homework at primary school?
She would have liked more homework at primary school because this would have helped her to adjust better to the demands of homework at secondary school. (1 mark)

6 Why would Mrs Smith like her daughter to have more homework?
Mrs Smith would like her daughter to have more homework because her daughter is intelligent and needs more challenging work than she is getting in class. (1 mark)

7 a) What does Daniel Wright mean when he says that his homework sessions are overseen?
Daniel means that homework sessions are supervised. An older pupil or teacher is always there to maintain discipline.
b) Do you think this is a good idea? Give your reasons.
Accept any sensible reasons for either opinion, possibly:
Yes:
i) It helps you to concentrate.
ii) It provides you with someone to consult if there is any problem.
iii) Everyone is in the same boat.
iv) A system like this ensures that you get down to doing the work without wasting time.
No:
i) It means that you have to work in a classroom atmosphere.
ii) The presence of others can be distracting.
iii) A system like this doesn't encourage personal responsibility.
iv) The silence in supervised sessions can be inhibiting. (2 marks)

8 How do some schools involve parents in checking that homework is done?
Schools have various ways of involving parents in checking that homework is done. Bellview School tells parents that it is their responsibility to check. Smithfield High requires parents to sign homework diaries each evening.   *(1 mark)*

9 In what way is Peter Miller's school "quite severe" when homework is not done?
If pupils at Peter Miller's school do not do their homework on time they are given a detention.   *(1 mark)*

10 Explain the meaning of these words as they are used in the main article:
   a) counterparts (paragraph one) – *pupils of the same age*
   b) sample (paragraph one) – *a random group used for testing purposes (so that conclusions could be made about the population as a whole)*
   c) disgruntled (paragraph four) – *displeased/disappointed/dissatisfied*
   d) conscientious (paragraph four) – *hardworking/diligent/determined to do their very best*
   e) vital (paragraph five) – *essential/extremely important*
   f) conceded (last paragraph) – *granted/had to admit*   *(3 marks)*

Extension activities

Additional questions

1 "Homework is vital to the learning process." (Elspeth Insch, Principal of King Edward VI Handsworth School for Girls). Do you agree or disagree? Give your reasons.

Research

1 Do you have homework? Would you like more or less? Why?

2 Using the two questions above that you have just answered, conduct a small survey among your classmates and write up your findings.

Writing

1 "Digging in books can be fun" (Emily Smith, ten). Have you ever really enjoyed working on a particular project or assignment, whether in class or at home? Write about what you were asked to do and why you enjoyed it so much.

2 Day schools could have supervised homework sessions after school just like boarding schools. Do you think this is a good idea? Explain.

3 Do you think that homework should be voluntary? Explain your answer.

NOW READ ON

Find and read some more newspaper articles about education. Write about whether you agree or disagree with the points being made, and explain your answer.

SPECIFIC SKILLS   additional comprehension questions; conducting a survey; writing up survey findings; personal writing; expressing and justifying a point of view

Monsoon

GENRE	children's fiction
READING STRATEGIES	skimming; scanning; detailed reading
QUESTION FORM	answering in own words
UNDERSTANDING TESTED	questions 3, 4, 6 – literal; questions 9, 10 – deductive; questions 1, 2, 5, 8 – inferential; question 7 – evaluative

1 How can you tell from the passage that the monsoon comes regularly to India every year?
You can tell that the monsoon comes regularly because Mr Panwallah goes to Worli beach at about the same time each year to see it coming. (1 mark)

2 Explain the meaning of: "The city was washed clean not only of the year's dirt but also of the summer's heat".
The monsoon rains cleaned the city in two ways: they washed away all the dust and rubbish that had accumulated in the streets and also cleaned the air by bringing with them a refreshing coolness. (2 marks)

3 How did Hari earn some extra pocket money on June 10th?
He earned pocket-money by helping to push cars and taxis out of the flood water. (1 mark)

4 In what ways did the monsoon make life much more difficult for the boys working at the Sri Krishna Eating House?
Accept any four:
i) They had more customers than ever.
ii) It was hard to get the cooking fire to light.
iii) The fire smoked and made them choke.
iv) Customers made the floors muddy.
v) When the boys ran errands they got soaking wet and couldn't dry off. (2 marks)

5 Why was it particularly difficult for Hari to sleep at night during the monsoon?
He had become used to sleeping in the open air in the park but had to stay indoors during the monsoon where it was unbearably hot. (1 mark)

6 What did Mr Panwallah do for a living?
He sold (and also repaired) clocks and watches. (1 mark)

7 In what ways was Mr Panwallah a good friend to Hari?
Mr Panwallah was a good friend in many ways. Accept any three:
i) He took an interest in Hari.
ii) He gave him treats.
iii) He took him to the beach to see the monsoon coming (and negotiated Hari's evening off with Jagu).
iv) He told him about the monsoon.
v) He welcomed Hari's visits to his shop. (3 marks)

8 Explain in what sense Hari was "locked up night and day" in the Sri Krishna Eating House.
Hari was not really locked up like a prisoner but he felt as if he was. This was because he couldn't get away from his work place at night (it was too wet to sleep in the park) and he couldn't get away during the day even when he had a spare moment because Mr Panwallah was ill so he had nowhere else to go. (1 mark)

9 What is the meaning of these words in the passage?
a) drenched (paragraph two) – *soaked*
b) dramatic (paragraph six) – *huge/really significant*
c) stalled (paragraph six) – *came to a standstill (through engine failure)*
d) receded (paragraph nine) – *went down/subsided* (2 marks)

10 Which word in the passage means "tumult"?
"Turmoil" (in paragraph two) means "tumult". (1 mark)

Extension activities

Additional questions

1 List everything that made Hari's evening at Worli beach so festive.

2 Hari was twelve years old. Why had he stopped feeling like a child?

3 What is the meaning of "overtime" (paragraph seven)?

4 How was the monsoon rain like "a great sheet" (paragraph four)? Explain the comparison.

5 How was the spray just like "a whiplash" (paragraph one)? Explain the comparison.

Writing

1 Describe the worst storm you have ever experienced. Remember to include vivid details of what you could see and hear and how you felt.

2 What is the best outing you have ever been on? What made it so enjoyable? Write about it.

Research

1 Use a dictionary to find the answer to these questions:
   a) What is a rupee?
   b) What is a dhoti?
   c) What is a sari?
   d) What is a Bombay duck? (Note: it is not a duck!)
   e) What is another word for Indian corn?
   f) How do you walk in Indian file?
   g) What is an Indian summer?

2 Look at a map of India.
   a) Find Bombay (where Hari worked).
   b) Find the ocean that stretches all the way to Africa (paragraph three).

NOW READ ON

Read more of *The Village by the Sea* and find out what happened to Hari and his friends.

SPECIFIC SKILLS   additional comprehension questions; descriptive writing; narrative account; evaluative writing; research and retrieval

The sword in the stone

GENRE	legend/children's fiction
READING STRATEGIES	skimming; scanning; detailed reading
QUESTION FORM	answering in own words; multiple choice
UNDERSTANDING TESTED	question 8 – literal; questions 3, 5 – deductive; questions 1, 4, 6, 7 – inferential; questions 2, 9, 10 – evaluative

1 What did Sir Ector mean when he asked Kay, "Do you think you're ready to take your place with the best in the land?"?
He was asking his son if he felt confident enough to compete against the most famous knights in Britain (either in single combat in jousts or in multiple combat in tournaments).
(1 mark)

2 Why was there a "hint of sadness" on Sir Ector's face when the decision was made to go to Canterbury?
Accept any one of the following:
i) Sir Ector was sad that his son was now an adult and his childhood days were over.
ii) Sir Ector suspected that Arthur's true identity would soon be revealed and his care of him would be at an end.
iii) Sir Ector was sad that the way of life he had known for the last sixteen years had come to an end.
(1 mark)

3 Sir Ector's old-fashioned style of speech is meant to reflect the ancient time in which he lived. Rewrite in up-to-date everyday English these speeches.
a) "I cannot name him to you yet but I think the day cannot be far away."
"I can't tell you his name yet but I think I'll soon be able to."
b) "I have in mind to take you to Canterbury."
"I've been thinking of taking you to Canterbury."
c) "Aye, I think the time is come."
"Yes, I think the time has come."
(3 marks)

4 Why did the knights "give way" when King Lot of Orkney approached the sword in the stone?
They gave way out of respect for the greatest fighter of them all. They all assumed he would be the one to pull the sword from the stone.
(1 mark)

5 "Since daybreak he had been showering poor Kay with instructions, warnings and good advice until the lad didn't know which way to turn." Explain why the word "showering" is a good word to use here.
The comparison between Sir Ector's constant reminders and a shower of rain is very effective. It is as if every separate instruction, warning, and piece of advice is a separate raindrop falling thick and fast on Kay's head, overwhelming him.
(1 mark)

6 Why did Sir Ector tell Arthur to put the sword back?
c) Sir Ector wanted to double-check what had happened.
(1 mark)

7 What made Arthur glad just "for a moment" that he had come to Canterbury as a squire and not as a knight? Explain.
The sight of King Lot's sword made Arthur pleased "for a moment" that he would not be taking part in any form of knightly combat. He realised that King Lot's sword had been marked by contact with his opponents. Squires were attendants who served knights but didn't themselves take part in contests. In due course, squires graduated to being knights.
(2 marks)

8 We hear eventually who Sir Ector's "master" was. Name him.
Sir Ector's master was Merlin.
(1 mark)

9 The sword in the stone is described twice in the passage:
i) ... a huge stone with an anvil embedded in it, and a sword plunged through the anvil into the rock beneath.

ii) The sword was there, its hilt sticking invitingly up out of some old block, like a woodcutter's axe. You would think that two different swords and stones were being described!

a) How does the sword seem quite different in the second description?
In the second passage, the sword doesn't seem to be buried so deeply in the stone. Its hilt is "sticking out invitingly".

b) How does the stone seem quite different in the second description?
The stone in the second passage is described casually as "some old block". In the first passage the stone is not only huge but it has a metal anvil completely buried in it.

c) Why has the author done this deliberately?
The first description is how all the knights and the kings saw the sword in the stone. The second description is how Arthur saw it. As he was the rightful King, the sword and stone presented no difficulty to him. He pulled out the sword easily. (3 marks)

10 "The old sword slid out easily with a gentle whisper like the rustle of silk." What makes this a good description?
(Accept any one of the following.) It's a good description because:
i) You can hear the gentle whisper itself in the sounds of the words chosen to describe it.
ii) The sound of the sword sliding out is compared with two sounds that we know about: a whisper and the sound that silk makes.
iii) It suggests how easily the sword came out. The "gentle whisper" conveys the idea of a minimum of effort, and the rustle of silk suggests the gentle movement with which Arthur removed the sword. (1 mark)

Extension activities

Additional questions

1 Look again at the second paragraph. How does Andrew Davies manage to suggest the noise and confusion of the scene?

2 What surprised Arthur when he saw King Bors for the first time?

3 What is the meaning of the words underlined below?
   a) Arthur gazed in awe
   b) ... existed only in stories and legends
   c) a bewildering rainbow of pennants
   d) a confusion of horses, beggars, pedlars ...
   e) ... he had little time for wizards and their prophecies

4 Why does Arthur call Sir Ector "Father" if he isn't his father?

5 Merlin came to Canterbury that day "for reasons of his own". What do you think those reasons were?

Writing

1 Write a lively description of a busy scene of your choice. Try to capture the sights and sounds, smells and movements so that it comes alive for your reader.

NOW READ ON

Read more of *The Legend of King Arthur* (or another version of the legend) and find out what happened to Arthur.

SPECIFIC SKILLS   additional comprehension questions; descriptive writing

Mid-term break

GENRE	poem
READING STRATEGIES	skimming; scanning; detailed reading
QUESTION FORM	answering in own words
UNDERSTANDING TESTED	question 8 – literal; questions 1, 2, 3, 4, 5, 6, 7, 9 – deductive; question 10 – evaluative

Note for teachers

Teachers will recognise that pupils will find this a powerful and moving poem. It is best read by the teacher with the class as a whole, with plenty of time afterwards for discussion. Some children may want to talk about their own experience of death within the family circle and their feelings about it. The teacher can then move carefully back to the poem and show how Seamus Heaney talks for all of us within the context of his brother's death.

Class teachers will best be able to judge when to introduce the Unit, depending on pupils' individual circumstances and when the subject would be too painful and immediate to broach.

1 Why do you think his teachers decided that it was best for Seamus Heaney to stay in the sick bay that morning?
   They felt he needed some privacy after hearing such bad news (so that he could cry, for example). They knew he wouldn't be able to concentrate in class.   (1 mark)

2 What does "close" mean in the first verse?
   "Close" means "end".   (1 mark)

3 Why was Seamus Heaney embarrassed when his hand was shaken?
   Accept one of the following:
   i) He was embarrassed because elderly neighbours were standing up as a mark of respect and shaking his hand. (It would normally be him having to show respect to his elders.)
   ii) He might also have been embarrassed by the display of emotion and sympathy and not have known how to respond.
   iii) Finding the house full of people (and his parents so upset) after taking so long to get home would have been hard to cope with. The formality would have been unfamiliar.   (2 marks)

4 What does "stanched" (sometimes spelt "staunched") mean in verse five?
   "Staunched" means that the bleeding had been stopped.   (1 mark)

5 In what ways could candles and snowdrops "soothe" a bedside?
   Accept any two:
   i) They would make the scene look calm and peaceful after the horrific accident.
   ii) They would look beautiful and take away some of the ugliness of the accident.
   iii) They would be a reminder of religion and spirituality, a sign that God was close to those who grieved, and that the little boy was at peace.   (2 marks)

6 In what ways did the bruise on the little boy's forehead resemble a poppy?
   (Accept any two points of comparison.) The bruise resembled a poppy in three different ways: in size, colour and shape.   (2 marks)

7 What is the meaning of "gaudy" as it is used in the seventh verse?
   "Gaudy" usually means bright/showy/vulgar, but here it means obvious/hideous/bright with blood.   (1 mark)

8 List all the sounds from this day in his childhood that Seamus Heaney remembers vividly.
   Accept any four:
   i) The school bells at the end of each lesson.
   ii) The sounds that the baby made.
   iii) The words of the neighbours (including Big Jim Evans).
   iv) The whispers explaining who he was.
   v) The agonised sighs of his mother.   (2 marks)

9 What time of year was it? How can you tell?
   It was February, half-way through the spring term. The snowdrops indicate this, as they flower early in the year. We also know that term began six weeks before. (1 mark)

10 What makes the last line of this poem so moving? Find as many reasons as you can to explain why we are left feeling so sad.
   Accept any two valid and sensitive responses. Pupils are likely to comment on the following in their own way:
   i) The economy of one line instead of three (as in every other verse).
   ii) The clear visual image of the tiny coffin that is hard to forget.
   iii) The first use of rhyme in the whole poem gives an extra resonance, a note of finality, almost a note of bitterness.
   iv) The simple monosyllables spell out the sad reality. (2 marks)

Extension activities

Additional questions

1 Why is "Mid-term break" a better title than "When my brother died"?

2 How does the use of the word "knelling" in verse one prepare us for the realisation that someone has died?

3 What do we learn about the mother's reaction to her young son's death?

4 Seamus Heaney's father had previously "taken funerals in his stride". What does that mean?

5 What do we learn about the reaction of friends and neighbours to the family's tragedy?

6 Do you think it was a good decision to leave Seamus Heaney in the sick bay all morning or would it have been better for him to be occupied? What would you have done if you were the teacher who had to make the decision?

Examining the poem

1 It has been said that Seamus Heaney writes this poem as an observer who notes the reactions of others but who feels nothing himself. Is this how you see him? Refer closely to the poem to support your comments.

2 "I don't think that Seamus Heaney should have written such a sad poem and published it for outsiders to read. It is a private family matter and nothing to do with anyone else." Do you agree or disagree with this reaction to "Mid-term break"? Give your reasons and describe your feelings as you read the poem and think about it later.

Writing

1 "Mid-term break" recalls one particular unforgettable day in Seamus Heaney's life. Write about an unforgettable day in your own life. You could choose an unforgettably sad or unforgettably happy day. Try to write down all the details that stay in your mind and that are important to your memory of the day.

NOW READ ON

Read more poetry by Seamus Heaney, especially poems about his childhood. Write about what you like and/or dislike about each poem.

SPECIFIC SKILLS   additional comprehension questions; expressing a point of view and justifying it; personal writing

UNIT
23

Moon landing

GENRE	children's science fiction
READING STRATEGIES	skimming; scanning; detailed reading
QUESTION FORM	answering in own words
UNDERSTANDING TESTED	questions 1, 3, 9, 10 – literal; questions 2, 4, 5, 6, 7 – deductive; question 8 – inferential

1 Why was it necessary for the ship-voice to wake Bethkahn from her long sleep?
The ship-voice woke Bethkahn because other beings were in the area and Bethkahn would have to decide what should be done. *(1 mark)*

2 What is "cryogenics"? (A dictionary will help you.)
"Cryogenics" is the practice of preserving at very low temperatures. *(1 mark)*

3 Explain why Bethkahn had not grown any older while she was in the cryogenic chamber (even though she had been in it for ten thousand years!).
Bethkahn had not grown any older in the chamber because, while she was inside it, time ceased to pass for her – her life was brought to a pause. *(1 mark)*

4 Why is the name "Galactic Academy" a good name for the college Bethkahn attended?
"Galactic" is the adjective from "galaxy" (a system of stars) and the college trained those who would later work on space exploration. *(1 mark)*

5 What is the meaning of an "initiation flight"?
This was Bethkahn's first flight as a trained junior technician on the starship. *(1 mark)*

6 Explain how studying "cause and effect" taught the ship to understand Bethkahn's feelings.
Although the ship couldn't feel what Bethkahn was feeling, it learned what situations were likely to move her in a particular way (make her sad or happy or frightened, and so on). *(2 marks)*

7 Explain the difference between:
a) fear and panic
Fear is the feeling you have when faced by danger or pain or other threatening situations. Panic is the frantic reaction to fear when you can't think how to cope.
b) desperation and despair
Desperation is a feeling of such hopelessness that you are driven to disregard danger and act recklessly. Despair is the total absence of hope, a settled feeling of hopelessness. *(2 marks)*

8 Why had the rest of the crew left the starship?
They had gone off to explore the beautiful turquoise blue planet they could see from the moon (while Bethkahn mended the stabiliser). *(1 mark)*

9 Why was it Bethkahn who had to stay behind to mend the stabiliser?
Bethkahn was the most junior technician on board and so this routine job fell to her. *(1 mark)*

10 Why was it vital to mend the stabiliser?
Without the stabiliser, the starship could not take off from the moon to resume its journey. *(1 mark)*

11 Why did Bethkahn find the waiting so difficult?
She found the waiting difficult because of the loneliness, the difficulty of measuring time, and also the worry about her colleagues on the planet's surface. *(1 mark)*

12 At the end of the extract, the ship is described as "her only friend". Explain how this contrasts with Bethkahn's earlier feelings about the ship.
Accept any reasonable response that identifies Bethkahn's emotions in the penultimate paragraph. Pupils are likely to comment on her feelings of "isolation and despair" and her hatred for the "useless metal artefact". There is also the earlier feeling of "power" that Bethkahn feels over the ship. Some pupils may comment on the passage of time indicated here ("through years of madness ...") to explain Bethkahn's changed feelings: after many years, she comes to realise that the ship is all she has left. *(2 marks)*

Extension activities

Additional questions

1 In what ways had Bethkahn "suffered" during the long absence of the crew?

2 Can you guess the name of the unknown planet on whose moon Bethkahn's starship landed?

3 There were two ways that the stabiliser could have been returned to working order.
   a) What were the two ways?
   b) Why was each one not possible?

4 Explain the meaning of the following words and expressions as they are used in the passage:
   a) elation   c) sheered off
   b) awesome   d) "paid me no heed"

5 This extract is the beginning of a story. Does it make you want to read on? Give your reasons.

Writing

1 Later in the story, we find that robot helpers do all the cleaning on the starship. If you could have a robot at home, what would you program it to be able to do? What would it look like?

2 Imagine that you have landed on planet Earth for the first time. Describe your first impressions.

Language

1 Antonyms are words that are opposite in meaning. Suggest antonyms for these words from the passage:
   a) transparent   d) joy
   b) junior   e) compressed
   c) elation

2 Homophones are words that sound the same but are spelt differently. Suggest homophones for each of the words below. Devise sentences to show how the words in each pair should be used.
   a) berth   f) told
   b) board   g) here
   c) metal   h) bear
   d) sheer   i) mind
   e) allowed

NOW READ ON

Read *Moonwind* by Louise Lawrence and find out if Bethkahn managed to mend the stabiliser and what had happened to Rondahl, Mahna and the rest of the crew.

SPECIFIC SKILLS   additional comprehension questions; imaginative (futuristic) writing; antonyms; homophones